HAUNTED
BRITAIN
AND IRELAND

HAUNTED BRITAIN
AND IRELAND

RICHARD JONES

with photographs from

THE FORTEAN PICTURE LIBRARY

MetroBooks

MetroBooks

An Imprint of Friedman/Fairfax Publishers

This edition published by Metrobooks by arrangement with New Holland Publishers (UK) Ltd

ISBN 1-58663-750-9

1 3 5 7 9 10 8 6 4 2

For bulk purchases and special sales, please contact:
Friedman/Fairfax Publishers
Attention: Sales Department
230 Fifth Avenue, Suite 700
New York, NY 10001
212/685-6610 FAX 212/685-3916

Visit our website:
www.metrobooks.com

Library of Congress Cataloging in Publication data available

Publishing Manager: Jo Hemmings
Project Editors: Elizabeth Mallard-Shaw, Kate Michell
Editorial Assistant: Anne Konopelski
Copy Editor: Cheryl Rose
Designer & Cover Design: Alan Marshall
Cartography: William Smuts
Index: Elizabeth Tatham
Production: Joan Woodroffe

Reproduction by Pica Digital Pte Ltd, Singapore
Printed and bound by Kyodo Printing Co (Singapore) Pte Ltd

Front cover: Ecclescrieg House, Fife, Scotland
Simon Marsden/The Marsden Archive
Back cover: Haunted House
Roger Brown/Fortean Picture Library

The HAUNTING

In screaming woods and empty rooms
or gloomy vaults and sunken tombs;
where monks and nuns in dust decay,
and shadows dance at close of day.

Where the bat dips on the wing
and spectral choirs on breezes sing;
where swords of ancient battles clash
and shimmering shades for freedom dash.

Where silver webs of spiders weave
and blighted lovers take their leave;
where curses lay the spirits low
and mortal footsteps fear to go.

Where death holds life in grim embrace
its line's etched on the sinners face;
where e'er the march of time is flaunted
Voices cry—"this place is haunted."

RICHARD JONES

CONTENTS

INTRODUCTION 8

1
LAND OF ARTHURIAN LEGEND
Cornwall, Devon, & Somerset 14

2
THE BLOODSTAINED LANDSCAPE WHERE ENGLAND WAS BORN
Dorset, Wiltshire, & Hampshire 24

3
THE COCKPIT OF THE NATION WHERE A KING'S FATE WAS SEALED
Herefordshire, Worcestershire, Warwickshire, Gloucestershire, & Oxfordshire 34

4
CAPITAL TERRORS AND HOME COUNTY HORRORS
London, Berkshire, Buckinghamshire, Bedfordshire, & Hertfordshire 44

5
SPECTRAL SHIPS, HISTORIC HILLS, AND ENGLAND'S MOST HAUNTED VILLAGE
Surrey, West Sussex, East Sussex, & Kent 56

6
THE WITCH COUNTIES
Essex, Suffolk, Norfolk, & Cambridgeshire 70

7
DEMONIC LORDS AND SATAN'S SORCERY
Northamptonshire, Leicestershire, Lincolnshire, Nottinghamshire, & West Midlands 84

8
SHADES OF TORTURE AMONG THE CRAGS
Derbyshire, Staffordshire, Cheshire, & Shropshire 94

9
MYSTERIOUS MOUNTAINS OF LEGEND
Wales 106

10
BANSHEES, BLARNEY, AND POOKAS OF THE EMERALD ISLE
Ireland 116

11
THE WINDSWEPT LANDS WHERE TERROR SAILED IN FROM THE SEA
North Yorkshire, Lancashire, Cumbria, & Northumberland 130

12
BLOODIED LAND OF KINGS AND CASTLES
Scotland 142

Recommended Reading 156 • Index 158
Acknowledgments 160

INTRODUCTION

On a bitterly cold and snowy day in April 2000, I climbed the muddy and uneven pathway that leads to the mysterious ruin of Dunstanburgh Castle, on the wild and windswept Northumberland coast. Standing on its crumbling walls, with the raging waves crashing onto the rocks below, I thought back over the previous nine months, during which I had journeyed all over Britain and Ireland in search of haunted locations. I thought of the people I had encountered, who all shared one thing in common—they had seen a ghost. Many of their stories were more or less the same. Characters, times, and locations changed, but the basic essence of the experience didn't. What was noticeable, however, was the plethora of ways in which people reacted to their experiences. Some felt it had somehow made them special, and were only too willing to talk about it, often at great length. Others were very matter of fact, almost blasé, about what had happened. The majority were somewhat embarrassed by the occurrence, and showed a marked reluctance to talk about something that they were convinced would single them out as being slightly eccentric.

During my research I also became aware of the "happened to a colleague" syndrome. These were the secondhand accounts related to me by the friends or family of those who had come into contact with ghosts. I found it rather amusing how these stories often climaxed with the statement that someone was "stone cold sober at the time," or the way in which the witness was often described as being "very pragmatic, the last person you'd ever expect to see this kind of thing." But there's the rub. Who is the kind of person who might see "this kind of thing" and, for that matter, what exactly is this "thing" that we call a ghost?

The Concise Oxford Dictionary says that "ghost" is "an apparition of a dead person which is believed to appear to the living, typically as a nebulous image," and I suppose that is how most of us would define it. When my first book on the subject, *Walking Haunted London*, was published, a question I was often asked was: "Do you believe in ghosts?" I became intrigued by my possible answer, since it forced me to think, "What is a ghost?" Surprisingly, in many years of collecting ghost stories, I had never really given much thought to this very basic question. I honestly do not believe that ghosts are the spirits of the dead coming back to haunt the living. My own opinion is that spirits, wraiths, revenants, specters, phantoms, call them what you will, are emotional imprints or

OPPOSITE: A phantom monk has been seen kneeling in silent contemplation amid the atmospheric ruins of Tintern Abbey in Monmouthshire.

BELOW: It is said that a ghostly Spanish soldier carries his head beneath his arm at Scotland's Eileen Donan Castle.

recordings that have been left on their surroundings, and that certain people, who we call "psychic," are simply more attuned to their wavelengths than the rest of us.

And yet, ghosts continue to mystify, fascinate, or outright terrify those who chance upon them. As I write these words, Hampton Court Palace has called upon the services of expert parapsychologist Dr. Richard Wiseman to see if he can explain why several visitors have taken ill and fainted at the spot where the ghost of Henry VIII's fifth wife, Catherine Howard, has long been said to appear. In addition to planning all-night vigils, throughout which thermal imaging cameras will be pointed at the spot, Dr. Wiseman plans to canvass around 600 visitors in an "attempt to pinpoint the character type most likely to report ghostly sightings." And yet the weight of evidence clearly demonstrates that ghosts do not appear to any specific type of person. They are elusive and baffling, often appearing before those who least expect to see them and, indeed, before the type of people who you would least expect to see them.

The Irish poet W. B. Yeats aptly summed up this spectral conundrum. Yeats was a great believer in spirits and, accompanied by his friend Lady Gregory, he devoted a great deal of time to collecting and publishing the supernatural experiences of the ordinary men and women of Ireland. In his biography of Yeats, G. K. Chesterton states that:

> … he used one argument which was sound, and I have never forgotten it. It is the fact that it is not abnormal men like artists, but normal men like peasants, who have borne witness a thousand times to such things; it is the farmers who see fairies. It is the agricultural laborer who calls a spade a spade, who also calls a spirit a spirit; it is the woodcutter, with no axe to grind, who will say he saw a man hang on the gallows and afterwards hang around it as a ghost.

Hundreds, if not thousands, of scientific attempts have been made to analyze and explain ghosts. The results are always inconclusive and the appliance of science to the tale of a haunting does, in my opinion, detract from what a ghost story really is. Few people can truly believe that Anne Boleyn's headless ghost gallops in a black carriage drawn by headless horses around the grounds of Blickling Hall in Norfolk. But to tell this story on a wild and stormy winter's night, as the wind and rain rattle the windows, with only a lone candle for light,

BELOW: The evocative ruins of Monmouth Castle, where Henry V was born.

is to summon up the true magic of the oral tradition. I venture that most people would rather hear the tale of Catherine Howard's screeching ghost racing along the Haunted Gallery of Hampton Court Palace than a bunch of statistics on light, humidity, and temperature from scientific studies that try to explain the phenomenon.

Ghost stories are a part of our heritage. They have no place in the cozy and certain world of academia, but belong in the children's playground, the local pub, and the popular imagination. Many of the stories do not stand up to scientific or, for that matter, historical analysis. And yet in an age of space travel, computers, and mass communication, the popularity of ghost stories is increasing rather than declining.

Assembled within this book you will find a very personal collection of such tales. From the outset my main problem was not what should be included, but rather what should be left out. I began with details of over 3,000 haunted places, of which I visited around 1,200. From those, I selected what I considered to be the most entertaining and varied tales. I was conscious of the fact that I could easily end up with a nebulous procession of white, pink, blue, and gray ladies parading across the pages, so in most cases I have tried to record the circumstances behind the hauntings. Aside from entertainment value, my only criterion for inclusion was that

ABOVE: This woodcut depicts the Lancashire witches, one of whom is accompanied by her devilish familiar.

BELOW: A depiction of what a ghost was expected to look like by the Pre-Raphaelite artist John Everett Millais.

need an explanation. I would argue that everyone needs a little mystery in his or her life, something to wonder at and ponder on.

My journey around the haunted realm ended on the windswept ramparts of Dunstanburgh Castle, watching the awesome might of the breaking waves deposit their foam around the crumbling crevices of the once mighty fortress. I thought of the men and women whose stories had become enshrined in legend; of castles sacked in war that have risen from the ruins, stronger and more imposing, only to be destroyed again when the passage of time brought new rivalries and new wars; of mysterious stone circles, whose origins are lost in the mists of time, and whose true purpose will never really be known. I repeated to myself Shakespeare's immortal words:

*We are such stuff
As dreams are made on, and our little life
Is rounded with a sleep.*

I thought of how utterly insignificant we human beings truly are in the greater scheme of things. Suddenly, I felt strangely at peace and very, very alone.

each location must be accessible to my readers. Thus, with very few exceptions, every location listed is open to the public. I apologize to the "modernists" of the genre for the exclusion of supermarket, launderette, or bingo hall hauntings. I am not a paranormal investigator but rather a collector of folklore. To me, ghosts belong on windswept moors, in old ruined castles, ancient inns, or stately homes. I have reported the stories more or less as they have been told to me, and have made few attempts to explain why they happen, being more than content to just accept that they do. I may find myself accused of being naive and a little too accepting in my approach, for we live in an age when everything appears to

RICHARD JONES

LAND *of*

ARTHURIAN LEGEND

"Therefore," said Arthur, *"take thou Excalibur, my good sword, and go with it to yonder water side, and when thou comest there, I charge thee throw my sword in that water, and come again, and tell me what thou there seest."*

FROM *LE MORTE D'ARTHUR* BY SIR THOMAS MALORY

CORNWALL, DEVON, & SOMERSET

The west of England is an area steeped in mystery. From the rugged cliffs and windswept landscapes of Cornwall, where timeless villages form one of the last bastions of Celtic England; to the wild wilderness of Dartmoor, with its tales of phantom hounds; and on to the rolling fields of Somerset, where legend says that Jesus himself once walked on "pastures green" and the so-called Isle of Avalon, in the mystical form of Glastonbury Tor, rises over a tranquil plain. Add to all this the tangible remains of nearly 5,000 years of history, and you have a potent brew from which fable and myth have woven a rich tapestry of legend and lore, that fires the imagination, and can still stir feelings of awe in even the

KEY

1. Dozmary Pool
2. St Senara's Church
3. Tintagel Castle
4. Warleggan
5. Berry Pomeroy Castle
6. Buckland Abbey
7. Dartmoor
8. Jay's Grave
9. St Thomas's Church
10. The Riverside Inn
11. The George and Pilgrim Hotel
12. Sedgemoor Battlefield

DOZMARY POOL
Bodmin Moor, Cornwall

Few roads venture into the wilderness of Bodmin Moor's windswept hinterland. The eerie remnants of prehistoric villages litter the haunting landscape; Celtic crosses lean wearily against the bleak and unforgiving terrain, while mysterious stone circles huddle together, jealously guarding their ancient secrets. Long-abandoned mine buildings stand gaunt against the skyline, their dark silhouettes often enveloped in a thick mist, lending them a sinister and ghostly air. It is a brooding,

PREVIOUS PAGES: The clifftop ruin of Tintagel Castle, the reputed birthplace of England's legendary King Arthur.

OPPOSITE: Dozmary Pool on Bodmin Moor, where King Arthur was brought to die.

fearsome place, and you feel its demonic influence the moment you set foot on its sodden carpet of swampy tussocks.

At the heart of the moor ripple the dark, leaden waters of Dozmary Pool, to the rock-strewn banks of which Sir Bedivere is said to have brought the dying King Arthur, and from where, according to Tennyson, came forth the arm "clothed in white samite" that caught Excalibur by the hilt, "brandish'd him three times, and drew him under in the mere."

At night a dark spirit is said to sit by its sullen waters, his despairing cries discernable over the wildest of autumn gales. He is the ghost of a stern and unpopular 17th-century magistrate, Jan Treagle. Some say that he murdered his wife and children, others that he used his position to acquire the rightful inheritance of a local orphan. As a result, his specter has been doomed to eternal torment. Night after night he must try to empty the bottomless pool with a perforated lamprey shell, while baying hounds snap at his ankles to ensure that he never falters at his impossible task.

ST. SENARA'S CHURCH
Zennor, Cornwall

❈ ❈ ❈ ❈ ❈ ❈ ❈ ❈ ❈ ❈ ❈ ❈ ❈ ❈ ❈

In the tiny and picturesque seaside village of Zennor, there stands a pretty and historic church dedicated to St. Senara. Tucked away in a side alcove is a chair that displays the scars which five hundred and more years of constant use have inevitably left behind. On its side is carved the figure of a mermaid, a symbol often used by the Church in the Middle Ages to illustrate the two natures of Christ.

Local legend, however, maintains that this figure commemorates an actual event from the parish's history, when the singing of a chorister named Matthew Trewhella enticed a mermaid ashore from the depths of the sea. Each Sunday she would sit at the back of the church, spellbound by his beautiful voice. One day, she could contain her infatuation no more and, luring him from the church, led him along the tiny stream that still babbles through the center of the village, and into the sea at nearby Pendour Cove. After that day, Matthew Trewhella was never seen again. But on warm summer evenings, if you stroll to

ABOVE: The mermaid chair in St. Senara's Church, Zennor.

the picturesque inlet now called "Mermaid's Cove," it is said that you will hear the two lovers, singing happily together, their voices rising from deep beneath the crashing waves.

TINTAGEL CASTLE
Tintagel, Cornwall

❈ ❈ ❈ ❈ ❈ ❈ ❈ ❈ ❈ ❈ ❈ ❈ ❈ ❈ ❈ ❈

Only ragged vestiges now survive of this once mighty fortress that, although not built until 1236, tradition holds was the birthplace of England's most legendary king—Arthur, son of Uther Pendragon. Its sullen mass of gray stone has been broken in two by the ceaseless pounding of the ocean beneath. Each year more and more of the rock face collapses into the raging waters. One day the remnants of the castle will follow, and its potent spell will be but a distant memory.

The hearsay of legend has added a goodly smattering of ghostly tales to the ruins and surrounding area. The ghost of Merlin is said to haunt the dark, dank cave in the bay below that bears his name. Such is its awesome atmosphere that few who venture into its icy interior, and gaze upon its fearsome black walls of jagged rock, ever dare linger for more than a few marrow-chilling moments.

Debate still rages over whether Merlin or Arthur ever set foot in this remote and rugged wilderness. However, in 1998, the discovery on the site of the "Arthnou Stone" sent waves of excitement rippling through the world of Arthurian belief. Its 6th-century Latin inscription translates as "Artognou father of a descendent of Col made this," and it has been suggested that it was the foundation stone for a much older fortress. The similarity between the names "Artognou" and "Arthur" provides an intriguing link between this place of windswept mystery and a possible real-life King Arthur.

But for the thousands of visitors from all corners of the globe who undertake the ankle-jarring romp to the clifftop ruins, no proof of Arthur's connection with the site is needed. For them this is a place of ancient enchantment, where history and fable cloud together, and the magic of Merlin casts a truly potent and mystical spell.

WARLEGGAN
Cornwall

In 1931, the Reverend F. W. Densham arrived to take up the incumbency of St. Bartholomew's church in the remote village of Warleggan. He was sixty-one years old, a thickset, square-jawed man, who had traveled extensively and was set in his ways. Within a year of his arrival, his autocratic style had so alienated his parishioners that they petitioned the Bishop of Truro to remove him from office. When this failed they simply boycotted his services, and each Sunday he would address a nonexistent congregation, resorting, it is said, to placing cardboard cutouts in the pews on which he wrote the names of past vicars. Week after week he would note poignantly in the register, "No fog, no wind, no rain, no congregation." When word of the feud leaked beyond the boundaries of the parish, the Reverend Densham became something of a celebrity and, by the 1950s, his Sunday congregation was often swollen by reporters from journals such as *Life*.

Reverend Densham's death in 1953 was as lonely as his life had been. He died on the staircase of the vicarage, where he lay undiscovered for two days. When his body was finally found, his arm was reaching for the bell rope, his last moments having evidently been spent attempting to summon the assistance of his alienated parishioners.

Reverend Densham's ghost has been seen on more than one occasion, wandering the overgrown pathway leading to the vicarage, and his fame is such that his story still draws curious visitors to the tiny and seemingly neglected church.

BERRY POMEROY CASTLE
Berry Pomeroy, Devon

The ancient and powerful de Pomeroy family arrived in Devon with the Norman Conquest, although the castle that bears their name dates only from the 15th century.

Legend holds that for their part in the religious rebellion of 1549, Edward VI ordered the seizure of their castle. But when his troops arrived to enforce the order, the two de Pomeroy brothers who held it donned their armour, blindfolded their horses, and spurred them over the ramparts, from where they crashed to their deaths at the feet of their astonished, would-be captors.

The building was then acquired by the King's Protector, Edward Seymour and, following his execution in 1552, became the abode of his son, also called Edward. The family extended the building, adding a magnificent manor house. But when the building was struck by lightning in 1685, the family lost interest in it, and by 1701 it had become a moldering ruin.

Today, the rambling ruins of the once mighty fortress perch eerily on a rocky throne above a wooded ravine, and several ghosts are said to wander inside its crumbling walls. A "blue lady" haunts the hollow shell of its splendid 16th-century manor house. She is said to be a daughter of the de Pomeroy family who, having become pregnant by her own father, smothered her baby the moment it was born, and has been condemned to wander the ruins in eternal remorse. But the eeriest part of the ruins is beneath the 15th-century Margaret Tower, and is reached by a twisting stone staircase that spirals down into a dank, dark dungeon, where a feeling of dreadful foreboding emanates from the moss-clad walls.

Here, the wicked Eleanor de Pomeroy imprisoned and starved to death her sister Margaret, because they both loved the same man and Eleanor was jealous of her sibling's beauty. Margaret's misty form appears in the depths of the tower, and many visitors have felt the cold chill of her unseen presence as she brushes by them on the dimly lit stairwell that leads to her eternal prison cell.

BUCKLAND ABBEY
Yelverton, Devon

Nestling in their peaceful woodland setting, the sleepy buildings of Buckland Abbey blend harmoniously into their

OPPOSITE: The eerie ruins of Berry Pomeroy Castle, where visitors often feel the cold chill of an unseen presence drifting past them.

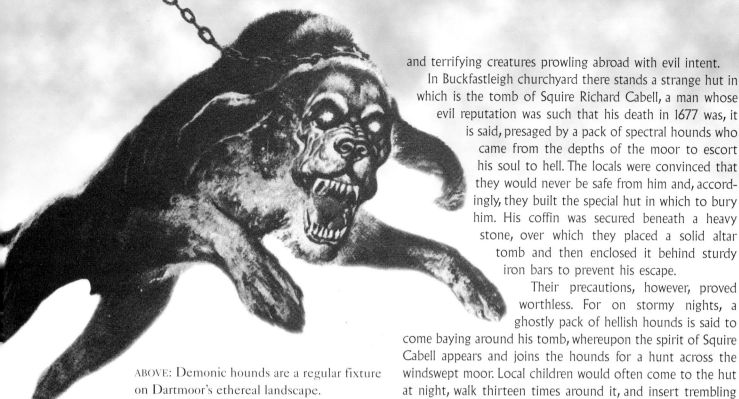

ABOVE: Demonic hounds are a regular fixture on Dartmoor's ethereal landscape.

and terrifying creatures prowling abroad with evil intent.

In Buckfastleigh churchyard there stands a strange hut in which is the tomb of Squire Richard Cabell, a man whose evil reputation was such that his death in 1677 was, it is said, presaged by a pack of spectral hounds who came from the depths of the moor to escort his soul to hell. The locals were convinced that they would never be safe from him and, accordingly, they built the special hut in which to bury him. His coffin was secured beneath a heavy stone, over which they placed a solid altar tomb and then enclosed it behind sturdy iron bars to prevent his escape.

Their precautions, however, proved worthless. For on stormy nights, a ghostly pack of hellish hounds is said to come baying around his tomb, whereupon the spirit of Squire Cabell appears and joins the hounds for a hunt across the windswept moor. Local children would often come to the hut at night, walk thirteen times around it, and insert trembling fingers into the keyhole to see if the evil squire would gnaw at them.

It was legends such as this that lured Sir Arthur Conan Doyle to Dartmoor in 1901. As he toured the lonely villages that surround the moor, and traversed its remote hinterland, absorbing its threatening atmosphere and gazing upon its

BELOW: Does the body of an 18th-century suicide lie beneath this mysterious grave?

surroundings, and no one who ventures here can deny that the whole foundation lies in a time warp.

In 1582, the abbey was purchased by Sir Francis Drake, who started a rebuilding program which, local tradition claims, took a mere three nights to complete because he invoked the assistance of the devil! As punishment for this demonic dabbling, Drake, it is said, has been condemned henceforth to drive a black hearse drawn by four headless horses across Dartmoor on moonless, windswept nights. The fearsome cortege is pursued by a spectral pack of baying hounds, their hellish howls carried upon the wild winds, as they seek the souls of unbaptized infants.

Inside the building is displayed the drum that is supposed to have been returned to Buckland Abbey on Drake's instructions, as he lay dying aboard his ship off Puerto Bello, Panama, in January 1596. The spirit of Drake is said to live on in this battered drum, and there is a tradition that its beat will be heard whenever England is in danger. It was heard on the eve of the Battle of Trafalgar, and again in 1939, when the specter of another war hung over Europe.

DARTMOOR
Devon

❉ ❉ ❉ ❉ ❉ ❉ ❉ ❉ ❉ ❉ ❉ ❉ ❉ ❉ ❉ ❉ ❉

With its bleak aura of desolation, prehistoric remains, grim prison, and malodorous mires, Dartmoor is a fearsome wilderness—even on the most pleasant summer's day. But when a keen wind howls across its bleak sedges, and a dank mist smothers the moor in its fetid embrace, it is a place where nightmares abound, and it is easy to imagine hideous

ABOVE: An aura of bleak desolation hangs over the windswept wilderness of Dartmoor.

boggy mires, he was accompanied by a young coachman named Harry Baskerville. Impressed by the aristocratic sound of the name, Doyle asked if he might use it, and thus was woven the backcloth against which Sherlock Holmes's most famous and spine-chilling adventure, *The Hound of the Baskervilles*, unfolded.

JAY'S GRAVE
Dartmoor, Devon

As you travel the road between Heatree Cross and Hound Tor, you come upon one of Dartmoor's most poignant monuments—the raised grave of Kitty Jay. Although little is known about the woman who supposedly lies here, tradition tells us that she was an 18th-century workhouse orphan who, having been ruined and deserted by a fickle lover, hanged herself and was buried at a crossroads with a stake driven deep into her heart, as was the custom in those days for dealing with suicides.

In 1860, her bones were discovered and buried in this wayside grave, on which for many years afterwards fresh flowers would mysteriously appear each morning. Even when the blizzards of winter had covered the moor with a thick blanket of snow, the flowers would appear, although no footprints were ever visible in the snow surrounding the grave. Today, there are frequent reports of a footless, female figure that is often seen eerily floating above the wayside grave of Kitty Jay.

ST. THOMAS'S CHURCH
Lapford, Devon

In the village churchyard at Lapford stands an intriguing memorial. It commemorates the Reverend John Arundel-Radford, a mid-19th-century vicar of the parish who, for reasons unknown, murdered his curate, but was acquitted by the jury at his subsequent trial on the grounds that they "had never hanged a parson, and weren't going to start now."

The murderous vicar returned to the bosom of his parish after his trial, where he continued with his ministry until his death in 1867. He left behind him a grieving widow, a modest estate, and the ominous threat that if he wasn't buried inside the church, he'd be back to haunt the village! However, in view of his past indiscretions, the authorities decreed that he must be buried outside the church and, true to his word, his ghost

ABOVE: Is this the sword that killed Thomas à Becket in December 1170?

BELOW: The 15th-century George and Pilgrim Hotel, Glastonbury, haunted by a medieval lovestruck monk and his admiring lover.

often paces the neighborhood, with a look of angry disdain upon its face.

There is also a tradition that the stone cross marking his grave will never stand upright so long as he remains outside the church. But stepping into the churchyard, you are at once struck by the bizarre and awkward angles at which virtually all the tombstones seem to lean—with the exception, that is, of the cross that stands erect, not leaning, over the grave of the Reverend John Arundel-Radford.

THE RIVERSIDE INN
Bovey Tracey, Devon

On an oak beam in the reception of this delightful hotel is the sword that was reputedly used to kill Thomas à Becket. The Tracey family, from whom the village takes part of its name, came to England with the Norman Conquest and acquired substantial lands in Devon. William Tracey was one of the four knights who, taking literally Henry II's outburst, "who will deliver me from this turbulent priest," murdered à Becket in Canterbury Cathedral, in December 1170. Returning to the family estates in Devon, he is said to have thrown the sword that dealt the fatal blow into the River Bovey. It was rediscovered three hundred years ago, when the water channel that now runs beneath the inn was being dug, and it has adorned the reception ever since. Opinion is divided over the sword's authenticity—which is now, obviously, impossible to prove—although there is overall general agreement that it is of the right age.

In addition to the intriguing relic, the inn is haunted. In the late 1990s, a lady visiting from America was woken one night by the overwhelming smell of burning. She placed damp towels beneath her door, but was still troubled by the acrid smell. She left her room to investigate, but could find no possible source of the smoke. When she complained of the experience to staff the next morning, they pointed out that it had been an exceptionally warm night, so no fires had been lit anywhere in the hotel.

THE GEORGE AND PILGRIM HOTEL
Glastonbury, Somerset

Glastonbury has been dubbed "the occult capital of England," and on the High Street stands

The George and Pilgrim Hotel, built in 1475 to provide hospitality to visitors to the nearby Benedictine abbey. Its superb freestone facade, with its mullioned windows, hides a veritable time capsule with low-beamed, narrow corridors, a winding old stone staircase, and at least two ghosts.

One is a spectral monk, who has been seen by many residents flitting about the dark corridors in the early hours of the morning, when the silence is broken only by the creaking of the hotel's ancient timbers as they settle. An elegant lady sometimes follows him on his wanderings, a look of longing admiration upon her pale, emaciated face. A regular guest at the hotel is a German medium, who has told the manager that the two were lovers in the days of the abbey. But due to the monk's vow of celibacy, their love was unconsummated, the frustration of which has left their spirits earthbound and doomed to wander The George and Pilgrim Hotel's snug and atmospheric corridors and passages.

In 1907, Frederick Bligh Bond was hired to excavate the 12th-century ruins of the abbey. In his endeavors, he uncovered two previously unknown chapels, plus sundry other important and impressive finds. In 1916, he revealed in his book, *The Gate of Remembrance*, that the spirits of long-dead monks, communicating through his friend, the medium John Bartlett, had guided his excavations. The church authorities were incensed by the disclosure and promptly sacked him, despite the obvious and proven success of his methods.

SEDGEMOOR BATTLEFIELD
Westonzoyland, Somerset

Sedgemoor must surely be one of England's most poignant battle sites. Two huge trees tower, sentry-like, over a memorial stone that commemorates the men of both sides who, "doing right as they saw it," died in the battle that was fought in the early hours of the morning of July 6, 1685, and who "lie buried in this field."

As dawn broke on that summer morning, James, Duke of Monmouth—an illegitimate son of Charles II—saw his hopes to take the throne of England from his uncle, James II, crushed in the mud of Sedgemoor field, along with the bodies of many of his dead and dying followers. Monmouth was executed on July 15, 1685, and this act was soon followed by the execution of many of his loyal supporters, as the infamous Judge Jeffreys meted out savage retribution at the notorious "Bloody Assizes."

The raw emotion of the battle, the dashed hopes, and appalling suffering have all left their mark on the surroundings, and ghosts from that long-ago conflict abound in the swampy field. Local farmers speak of spectral horsemen seen racing across the marshy expanse, or tell of disembodied voices that call to startled witnesses from across the River Carey, urging them to "Come over." They talk of Monmouth's shivering shade, doomed to reenact his cowardly escape from the field of battle when—it is said—he outran his comrades by an incredible distance.

But the most tragic wraith to haunt this evocative spot is that of a young girl, whose lover was captured by the Royalist troops. Knowing him to be a renowned athlete, the soldiers promised to spare his life if he could run as fast as a galloping horse. When the boy had met the challenge, the soldiers gunned him down in cold blood as his sweetheart looked on. In her sorrow, she drowned herself in the River Carey, and her phantom periodically returns to the site, where she glides along the route of her lover's last run. The thundering of a horse's hooves often accompanies her weary vigil, and the desperate panting of an invisible runner, coupled with a cold blast of air, have all been known to alarm even the most skeptical visitors who find themselves standing on Sedgemoor field as twilight creeps across the surrounding countryside.

ABOVE: James, Duke of Monmouth, whose shivering shade repeats his cowardly escape from the battlefield of Sedgemoor every year.

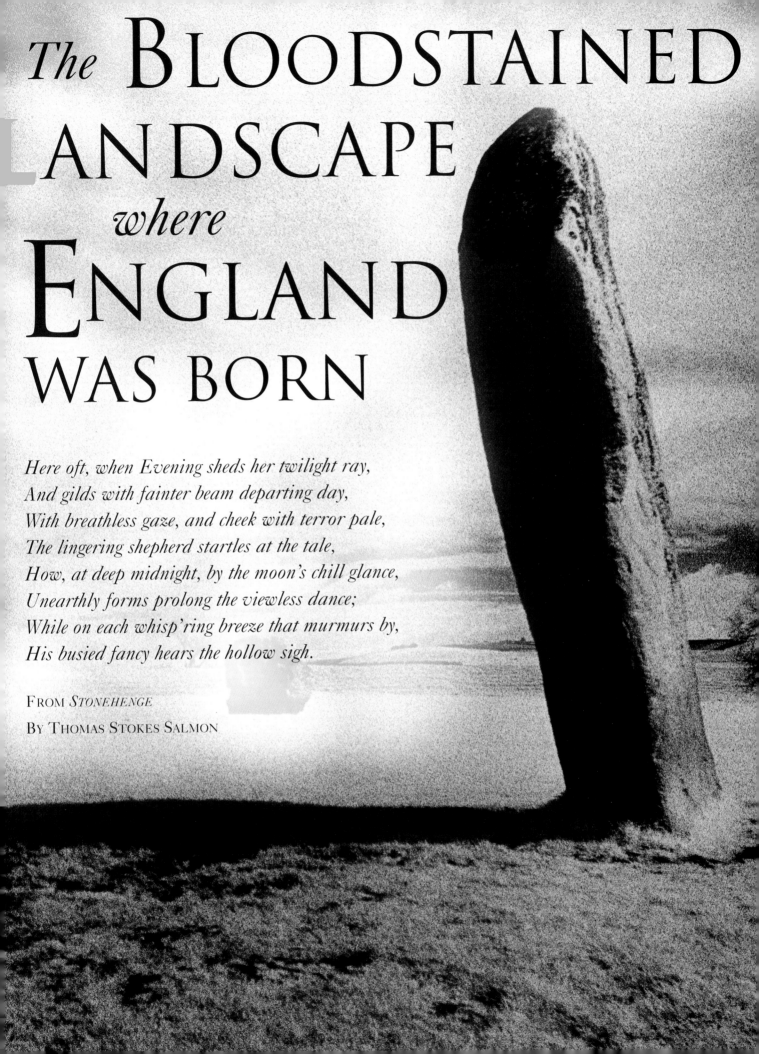

The BLOODSTAINED LANDSCAPE *where* ENGLAND WAS BORN

Here oft, when Evening sheds her twilight ray,
And gilds with fainter beam departing day,
With breathless gaze, and cheek with terror pale,
The lingering shepherd startles at the tale,
How, at deep midnight, by the moon's chill glance,
Unearthly forms prolong the viewless dance;
While on each whisp'ring breeze that murmurs by,
His busied fancy hears the hollow sigh.

FROM *STONEHENGE*
BY THOMAS STOKES SALMON

DORSET, WILTSHIRE, & HAMPSHIRE

Dominated by the vast chalk lands of Salisbury Plain, this legendary landscape once formed the core of the Saxon kingdom of Wessex where, under the leadership of Alfred the Great, England was born a little over 1,100 years ago. But long before the days of Alfred, a mysterious people cast their shadow across the area and the relics they left behind still baffle and amaze us today, some 3,000–4,000 years later. They carved strange figures and white horses into the chalk hillsides, and built earthworks that later generations would find so impossibly massive that they would attribute their construction to the devil. Most impressive of all, however, are the two great stone temples that they left at Avebury and Stonehenge. The magic of these temples draws visitors from all over the world to gaze in wonder at places of worship that date from the dawn of time.

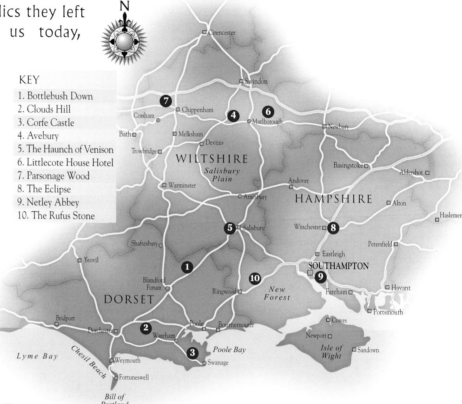

KEY
1. Bottlebush Down
2. Clouds Hill
3. Corfe Castle
4. Avebury
5. The Haunch of Venison
6. Littlecote House Hotel
7. Parsonage Wood
8. The Eclipse
9. Netley Abbey
10. The Rufus Stone

BOTTLEBUSH DOWN
Near Sixpenny Handley, Dorset

In 1924, Mr. R. C. Clay, an archeologist who was in charge of excavations at a Bronze Age site near Christchurch, was driving home one night along a highway which runs by Bottlebush Down, when he suddenly became aware of a man

PREVIOUS PAGES: The gods that our ancestors worshiped have never really departed from Europe's largest Stone Circle at Avebury.

OPPOSITE: Bottlebush Down, where England's oldest ghost rides across the green expanse in the fading light of day.

on a galloping horse racing alongside his car. The man wore a long flowing cloak, his bare legs spurred his horse on without bridle or stirrups, and he was brandishing some form of weapon, which he waved angrily above his head. As Mr. Clay looked on in puzzled astonishment, the horse and rider suddenly vanished into the burial mound on Bottlebush Down. Not believing the evidence of his own eyes, and determined not to dismiss the figure as something so unscientific as a ghost, the archeologist returned to the spot several times over the next few weeks. But having ruled out tricks of the light, optical illusions, or any other scientific possibility, he was forced to admit, grudgingly, that he was one of a long line of people to have witnessed the appearance of Bottlebush Down's spectral horseman.

Although today the area is remote and isolated, there is ample evidence to suggest that it was once a thriving hub of activity. The number of low, round burial barrows that litter its landscape suggests a sizable population 2,000–3,000 years ago. An immense earthwork, stretching for nearly six miles, and known as the "Cursus," must at one time have been heavily garrisoned, and was later a crossing point for the Roman road that connected Salisbury with Badbury. While the phantom horseman—whose galloping wraith has appeared to shepherds tending their flocks, cyclists returning home across Bottlebush Down in the fading light of day, and walkers out enjoying an evening stroll in the country air—could be a vestige of any one of the ancient peoples who lived here, Mr. Clay's specialist training enabled him to date the figure as being of the late Bronze Age. This means that, whoever he may have been in life, in death the warlike, galloping wraith has possibly achieved the distinction of being England's oldest ghost!

CLOUDS HILL
Bovington, Dorset

This whitewashed cottage, ensconced behind a tall screen of rhododendron, was little more than a ruin when Thomas Edward Lawrence, best remembered the world over by the sobriquet "Lawrence of Arabia," purchased it in 1925. Over the next ten years, he carried out extensive renovations, finished his autobiographical history *Seven Pillars of Wisdom*, and entertained such literary luminaries as Thomas Hardy, George Bernard Shaw, and E. M. Forster—whose description of Lawrence's home as "a primitive little house, curiously welcoming with its log fires and windy gramophone" perfectly describes its ambience.

In 1935, Lawrence left military service and retired to Clouds

dead—killed when he swerved to avoid two boys who had strayed into the path of his powerful Brough Superior motorcycle. But the emotions expressed in the letter to Lady Astor have proved prophetic, for his ghost, resplendent in swirling Arab dress, was soon seen entering his beloved cottage at dusk. Furthermore, the distinctive roar of his Brough Superior, racing along the local roads in the dead of night, has been heard by many who reside in the vicinity of the tiny cottage where "Lawrence of Arabia" found the peace that had eluded him for so long, but which—physically at least—was to be so short-lived.

CORFE CASTLE
Wareham, Dorset

Impressively situated on its lofty throne and protected by steep cliffs, this once vast fortress is now little more than a hollow shell. Having crossed the stone bridge that spans its deep moat, you find yourself wandering amid stark, monolithic columns, or meandering through narrow corridors, where ancient walls lean towards you at strange, almost threatening angles.

Although William the Conqueror began the castle, it was King John who turned it into the Royal Palace, the melancholic ruins of which survive today. During the English Civil War, the redoubtable Lady Bankes defended it until she was betrayed by one of her own garrison. When the Parliamentary soldiers gained possession of the building, they set about destroying

Hill, his contentment being such that in the May of that year, he wrote to Nancy Astor, exclaiming, "Nothing would take me away. It is an earthly paradise and I am staying here." Five days after recording those sentiments, he was

ABOVE: The ghost of "Lawrence of Arabia" still rides around the Dorset countryside on a phantom Brough Superior motorbike!

the edifice. They toppled its mighty walls, undermined its foundations until—and within a short period of time—nothing but the hollow shell that is there today remained.

An aura of mystery soon descended over the bare ribs of the once regal pile, as people began to whisper of ghostly encounters within the moldering ruins. Strange, flickering lights were seen moving about the ramparts at night. The heartrending sobs of a weeping child were heard in a cottage that abuts the rocky knoll on which the castle stands. But the most persistent of all the specters that haunt the robust remnants is the headless "white lady," whose shimmering shade chills the blood of those who chance upon her, and sets them shivering and shaking until she turns and drifts slowly away, fading into nothingness as she goes.

AVEBURY
Avebury, Wiltshire

Ancient banks and ditches, almost a mile in circumference, encircle much of the tiny village of Avebury. On them stands Europe's largest stone circle or, to be more precise, several stone circles, dating from between 4,000 and 2,400 BC. It is a place steeped in mystery, from which the gods that our ancestors worshiped have never really departed.

In the 14th century—probably acting on the instructions of the church—the villagers began to topple the megaliths and bury them in deep pits. This zealous act of vandalism angered whatever spirits lurked within the stones, and they exacted vengeance on at least one of their assailants. When the monoliths were rediscovered in 1938, several 14th-century coins and sundry other items were found buried beneath one of them. The archeologists had little problem identifying the last owner of the relics, because his grinning skull was leering back at them from beneath the colossus! It would seem that a tragic accident had caused the stone to topple onto the unfortunate man, crushing him to death. The sheer weight of the mammoth stone made removal of the body impossible, so his workmates had simply left him interred beneath it. Since the tools found alongside his bones suggested he was a barber-surgeon, the murderous megalith became known as the "Barber Stone" and today stands proud and erect upon its original site.

Throughout the 18th and 19th centuries, many surviving stones were broken up for use in the construction of various buildings in the neighborhood, and stories abound of close escapes from similar accidents. A cobbler who had been working beneath one of the stones on the Sabbath had only just walked away when it suddenly fell over, crashing onto the spot where he had just been sitting. A parish clerk, having sheltered from a violent storm beneath one of the megaliths, was horrified when, as he headed for home, a bolt of lightning smashed into the stone and blew it to pieces. Evidently the guardians were still displeased! Today, people talk of seeing strange, ghostly figures moving about the stones at night, or of hearing singing where no human forms are to be seen.

The stones still inspire feelings of wonder and dread, and no one who gazes upon them for the first time, or arrives to find them rising ghost-like from a swirling mist on a crisp winter's morning, can fail to be moved by their magic.

THE HAUNCH OF VENISON
Salisbury, Wiltshire

Parts of this old inn—with its low beams, intricate carvings, and sloping floors—date back almost seven hundred years. It backs onto the tiny graveyard of St. Thomas's church, from where a lady clad in a brilliant white shawl is often seen gazing down upon startled onlookers from the inn's upper windows. She may be the playful ghost that has a penchant for playing practical jokes on bemused staff, several of whom have found that crockery, which they have painstakingly stacked in the kitchen, has been moved back to the bar when their backs were turned!

But the tavern's most persistent haunting is the sound of ghostly footsteps heard at night pacing around the upstairs

BELOW: The bare ribs of Corfe Castle are the ghostly domain of a headless white lady.

rooms between 11.30p.m. and midnight. During renovation work, a secret alcove was found behind one of the pub's old fireplaces. Inside, workmen were horrified to discover a severed human hand and a yellowed, marked playing card. It has since been suggested that the phantom footsteps, which staff say sound agitated and anxious, may be the result of a gruesome justice meted out to a former customer who was caught cheating during a game of cards.

BELOW: The impressive Great Hall at Littlecote House, where a gruesome 16th-century murder has caused a tragic specter to wander for evermore.

LITTLECOTE HoUSE HOTEL
Littlecote, Wiltshire

This gabled, Elizabethan manor house, with its Great Hall, long gallery, period paneling, and hanging tapestries, is now a luxurious hotel. It is hard to believe that in 1575 a gruesome crime took place here which would have, had it not been for the deathbed confession of a midwife named Mrs. Barnes, remained just one of the many dark secrets that a building of this antiquity inevitably keeps hidden from prying eyes.

Mrs. Barnes related to an astonished magistrate, Mr. Anthony Bridges, how on one rainswept November night in 1575, a stranger had come to her house and told her that a lady of quality needed her professional services. When the midwife agreed to assist, she was blindfolded and taken to a country house. The blindfold removed, she found herself in a large room, where on a bed lay a masked lady in the latter throes of labor.

The midwife went about her business, but no sooner had she delivered the baby than the man snatched it from her hands and, despite the horrified screams of the exhausted mother, threw the infant onto the fire, where he held it down with the heel of his boot until it was dead. The horror-stricken midwife, realizing that there might well be an inquiry into the infanticide, cut a small square of fabric from one of the bed curtains before she was led, blindfolded once more, from the room and returned to her own house.

She kept secret what she had witnessed until she knew she was dying, and felt the need to make her contrition and bring the murderer to justice. Suspicion immediately fell upon "Wild" Will Darrell, the owner of Littlecote. He was duly arrested, and a search of the house revealed a hole in one of the bed curtains, into which the piece of fabric given to the magistrate by Mrs. Barnes fitted exactly. But at his subsequent trial, Darrell was acquitted of the crime, amid speculation that he had bribed the judge, Sir John Popham.

Soon afterward, Darrell was riding his horse in Littlecote Park, when the ghost of the murdered baby is said to have suddenly appeared before him, causing his horse to throw him, the resultant fall breaking his neck. The gate by which the accident happened is still called "Darrell's Stile," and his ghost has often been seen there.

Meanwhile, speculation has long raged over the identity of the unfortunate mother. "Wild" Will was so named because of his amorous exploits, and he had numerous mistresses, both married and single. Some say she was the wife of Sir Henry Knyvett, others that she was a Miss Bonham, or even that she was

ABOVE: The picturesque village of Castle Coombe, where disembodied voices are heard on winter evenings in the woods nearby.

his own sister. But whatever her identity, her ghost is said to walk the corridors and rooms of Littlecote, wearing a pink nightdress and holding the murdered baby in her arms. An indelible bloodstain was long reputed to appear in the "haunted chamber" where the murder occurred, and many is the person who has been woken by the sound of terrified screams echoing through the corridors of the old house in the early hours of the morning.

PARSONAGE WOOD
Castle Coombe, Wiltshire

Massive trees rise majestically above the sleepy village of Castle Coombe, cradling its honey-colored stone cottages in a protective embrace that keeps the contemporary world firmly at bay. In summer, when the twittering of the birds and the babbling waters of the Bybrook lend the area an aura of timeless tranquillity, to stroll beneath the leafy boughs of Parsonage Wood on a warm August evening is to feel centuries removed from the pressures of the modern age. But when the dark cloak of a winter's night descends across the wood, only the extremely brave or exceedingly foolhardy are to be found upon its muddy paths. Many people have been alarmed by the sound of disembodied voices chattering excitedly in the darkness around them. As they reach a fevered crescendo, the voices are joined by the groans of someone apparently suffering intense pain. Suddenly a loud scream rends the air, and then all goes quiet. No one knows for sure what lies behind the strange phenomena, but few who experience it ever venture into Parsonage Wood again.

THE ECLIPSE
Winchester, Hampshire
❧ ❧ ❧ ❧ ❧ ❧ ❧ ❧ ❧ ❧ ❧ ❧ ❧ ❧

On September 2, 1685, Dame Alice Lisle stepped through an upstairs window of this ancient hostelry, placed her old and weary neck upon a wooden block, and was beheaded. Her crime was to have given shelter to two rebels fleeing the bloody aftermath of the Monmouth uprising. She was sentenced to death at the infamous "Bloody Assizes" by the notorious "Hanging Judge" Jeffreys. Jeffreys had wanted Lisle to be dragged on a hurdle through the streets of Winchester, and then burned at the stake. But King James II, fearful of the reaction to such a punishment from the people of Hampshire, commuted her sentence to a simple beheading. And so Lisle's last night was spent in an upper room of The Eclipse, repose made impossible by the sounds of the scaffold being erected, hard against its walls.

Once the executioner had finished his bloody business, Lisle's body was conveyed to its final resting place in Ellingham churchyard. The mournful cortege was followed by hundreds of ordinary men and women, walking in silent procession to show their disapproval at her unjust fate. Since then, Dame Alice Lisle has returned time and again to the timbered tavern where she spent that last troubled night. Her sudden appearance has startled staff and customers alike as, clothed in a gray woolen dress, she watches them silently from dark recesses. Her sad and

solemn specter is now regarded as nothing less than the oldest and most distinguished resident of this atmospheric and timeless establishment.

NETLEY ABBEY
Near Woolston, Hampshire
❧ ❧ ❧ ❧ ❧ ❧ ❧ ❧ ❧ ❧ ❧ ❧ ❧ ❧

The romantic ruins of this Cistercian abbey, which was founded in 1239 but converted in the 16th century to a palatial private house, huddle in a wooded dell near Southampton Water. The sprawling foundations are a vivid testimony to how splendid the building must once have been. Somber passages meander between gloom-laden walls, delivering visitors into dark, vaulted rooms, where the chimneys of massive fireplaces stretch heavenward, and an eerie weariness hangs heavy in the air.

At night it is said that the hallowed ruins are protected by the ominous specter of a solitary monk, whose task is to ensure that harm befalls anyone who attempts to damage the ancient fabric.

In the early years of the 18th century, the site was sold to a builder named Walter Taylor, who intended to dismantle it and use the stone elsewhere. However, before he could begin work, the phantom monk appeared to him in a dream and warned him of dire consequences should he continue with his task. Dismissing the dream, Taylor began demolition the next morning, whereupon a huge block of stone crashed onto his head and killed him instantly.

ABOVE: Dame Alice Lisle was condemned to be burned at the stake by the notorious "Hanging Judge" Jeffreys, but King James II commuted the sentence to beheading.

LEFT: A plaque in Winchester marks the spot where Dame Alice Lisle was beheaded in 1685.

SITE OF OLD MARKET HOUSE. PLACE OF EXECUTION OF LADY LISLE. 1685. IN THE ROADWAY.

THE RUFUS STONE
Minstead, Hampshire

❊ ❊

In 1087, William II—known as "Rufus" because of his ruddy complexion—inherited the throne of England from his father, William the Conqueror. He was not a popular king, and his reign was marred by constant uprisings and private wars waged by the Norman barons, who favored his elder brother Robert's claim to the Crown. In 1088, Robert organized a mass revolt against his sibling, forcing William to rely upon the support of his "brave and honorable" English subjects. In return, William promised to relax the crippling taxes that the Conquest had foisted upon them, and to abolish the hated Forest Laws. With his subjects' help, William successfully quashed the rebellion, and then promptly went back on his word by increasing taxes and enforcing the Forest Laws more harshly.

Universally despised by his subjects, William arrived in the New Forest on August 2, 1100 to enjoy an afternoon of hunting with seven trusted companions. At around seven o'clock in the evening the party split up, the king staying with Sir Walter

Tyrrel. When the rest of the group next saw William, he was dead, an arrow protruding from his breast.

Tyrrel swore it had been a dreadful accident, and that the arrow had glanced off a tree and hit the king. He chose, however, not to face the consequences and fled the country, stopping to wash his bloodstained hands in the pond at Castle Malwood, the waters of which were subsequently said to turn crimson every August 2. William's companions raced off to secure their estates against the vagaries of a new regime, and so it was left to Purkis, a poor charcoal burner, to transport the king's body to Winchester. As the wooden cart bounced along the rough roads, it is said to have left a trail of blood that William's ghost has been condemned to follow every anniversary since his death. His silent journey begins in the forest glade where the Rufus Stone now stands, marking the solemn spot where, on one summer's eve, a tragic accident, murder, or even—it has been suggested—human sacrifice, ended the thirteen-year reign of the tyrannical "Red King."

THE COCKPIT *of the* NATION *where a* KING'S FATE WAS SEALED

And travelers now, within that valley,
Through the red-litten windows see
Vast forms, that move fantastically
To a discordant melody,
While, like a ghastly rapid river,
Through the pale door
A hideous throng rush out forever
And laugh—but smile no more.

FROM *THE HAUNTED PALACE*
BY EDGAR ALLAN POE

HEREFORDSHIRE, WORCESTERSHIRE, WARWICKSHIRE, GLOUCESTERSHIRE, & OXFORDSHIRE

The mark of history is upon the counties that stretch westward from Oxfordshire to Herefordshire. It is a varied landscape, both physically and psychically. Oxford, with its dreaming spires and scholarly atmosphere, was chosen by Charles I as his headquarters during the dark years of the English Civil War, and several important skirmishes took place among the fertile valleys and sky-swept hills to the west of the city—an area that has long been known as "the nation's cockpit." These historic battles have, in turn, left an ethereal mark upon the landscape, and there are numerous accounts of ghostly Cavaliers and Roundheads still battling on, long after the conflict was settled with the beheading of Charles I in 1649. Today, this historic country-side is a magnet for people looking for some of England's most beautiful and tranquil surroundings.

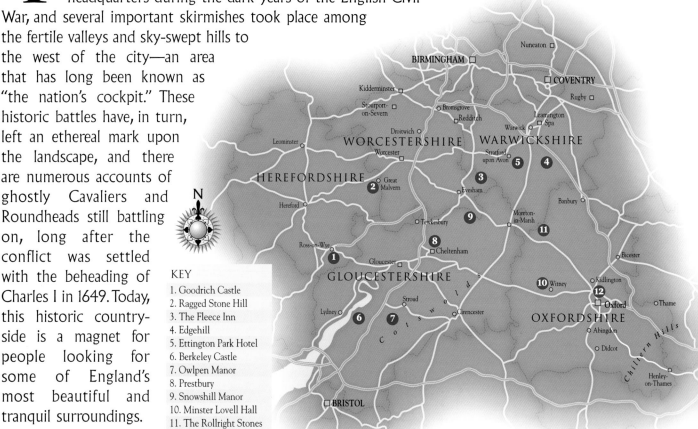

KEY
1. Goodrich Castle
2. Ragged Stone Hill
3. The Fleece Inn
4. Edgehill
5. Ettington Park Hotel
6. Berkeley Castle
7. Owlpen Manor
8. Prestbury
9. Snowshill Manor
10. Minster Lovell Hall
11. The Rollright Stones
12. St John's College

GOODRICH CASTLE
Goodrich, Herefordshire

The massive ruins of this red sandstone castle, which stand on a wooded, rocky spur overlooking the tranquil waters of the River Wye, are pitted with numerous nooks and crannies that

PREVIOUS PAGES: In November 1990, Derek Stafford photographed the floodlit graveyard in the village of Prestbury. He was astonished when the figure of a monk mysteriously appeared in one of his developed prints.

exude an aura of tragic mystery. The oldest part of the fortress is the stone keep, built in the 12th century, when the castle was an important bastion on the border of England and Wales. Enlarged over succeeding centuries, the castle last saw action during the Civil War, when, as a Royalist stronghold, it found itself under relentless bombardment as Cromwell's troops attempted to breach its mighty walls with 200-pound cannonballs fired from the aptly named mortar, "Roaring Meg."

During the siege, Alice Birch, the niece of a Parliamentarian officer, took refuge in the castle with her Royalist lover, Charles Clifford. When it became apparent that the fortress would not withstand the bombardment for much longer, Clifford and his

young lover mounted his horse and, under cover of darkness, spurred the beast out of the castle and broke through the Roundhead ranks. Unfortunately, when they arrived at the muddy banks of the River Wye, they didn't realize that heavy rains had dangerously swollen its waters. As they attempted to cross ithe river's raging torrents, their horse lost its footing, and they were swept away to their deaths. Such was the trauma of their desperate bid for freedom that their bedraggled, earthbound wraiths have been seen on stormy nights, urging a phantom horse into the River Wye. Their poignant specters are also occasionally seen staring sadly from the ruined ramparts.

RAGGED STONE HILL
Great Malvern, Worcestershire

The twin peaks of this brooding undulation are the haunt of a lustful friar from Little Malvern priory who, tortured by remorse, confessed his "human passion" to his prior.

ABOVE: The massive ruins of Goodrich Castle, from which the bedraggled specters of two 17th-century lovers attempt an annual escape.

Despite being guilty of the same offense, the pompous cleric condemned his underling to a penance of crawling up the rough side of Ragged Stone Hill on his hands and knees, day in and day out. The friar eventually grew exasperated by the enormity of the sentence and, in a fit of insane anger, is said to have stood upon a peak and hurled a curse upon the church and anyone upon whom the shadow of the somber pinnacles should fall. His curse cast, he stretched out his arms and fell to the ground dead. For those who might feel temped to dismiss the tale as idle legend and to stroll boldly beneath its menacing silhouette, consider the fates of the Duke of Clarence, Richard III, the Princes in the Tower, Henry VI, Cardinal Wolsey, and Anne Boleyn—all of whom wandered beneath its nebulous reach shortly before fate heaped tragedy or ignominy upon them.

THE FLEECE INN
Bretforton, Worcestershire
❧ ❧

This delightful, timber-framed hostelry was originally a medieval farmhouse, and remained as such until the Taplin family applied for an innkeeper's license in 1848. It has changed little since then, due largely to the fact that it remained in the same family until the death of Lola Taplin in 1977. On the hearths by the two fireplaces, you can still see several curious circles, known as "witch marks," that date back to a more superstitious age, when it was believed that the sinister sisterhood could enter a house via the chimney. Each night, prior to retiring to bed, successive householders would draw three round chalk marks upon the hearth to ensure that if a witch descended, she would be trapped within the circles until morning, when the day's first light would weaken her powers, and she would flee from the house. The frequency with which successive residents drew these marks has left indentations in the stone of the hearths at the Fleece Inn.

While witches are kept out, no such "marks" apply to ghosts, and it is generally accepted that the spirit of Lola Taplin haunts the Fleece. This formidable lady ran the pub on her own for the last thirty years of her life and was fond of informing customers, in no uncertain terms, that they were honored to be drinking in her home. She always insisted that guests only partook of alcoholic beverages, and thus food was banned. Shortly after her death the rule was relaxed, and Lola appears to have shown her objections in a very direct manner. A customer had reportedly placed his sandwich box on one of the tables when it was suddenly lifted into the air by an invisible hand and flung to the floor, scattering the contents everywhere. On other occasions, ghostly footsteps have been heard plodding around the property, while an unseen force has been known to hurl small objects in what appears to be a phantom fit of pique.

EDGEHILL
Kineton, Warwickshire
❧ ❧

On October 23, 1642, the first major clash of the Civil War was fought at Edgehill, where Charles I, with an army of 13,000 men, had blocked the retreat of a slightly smaller Parliamentarian force commanded by Robert Devereaux, Earl of Essex. The early advantage went to the Royalist army until Charles's nephew, Prince Rupert of the Rhine, squandered it with an ill-advised cavalry charge that left the infantry exposed to an enemy attack. In the fierce hand-to-hand combat, the Roundheads succeeded in capturing the royal standard and killing its bearer, Sir Edmund Verney (see page 53). A Royalist cavalry officer, Captain John Smith, spotted a group of enemy troops making off with the colors. He charged after them, killed one, wounded another, and, as the others fled, retrieved the standard and returned it to the king—with Verney's hand still clasped around it!

Fifteen hundred men lost their lives that October day and, with the outcome of the battle indecisive, both sides were quick to claim the victory. The truth is that the advantage probably did go to the king's army, and had Charles then chosen to march on London, he might well have altered the course of history. But so appalled was he by the carnage of this, his first battle, that he was unable to concentrate on military strategy, and opted instead to head straight for Oxford, where he established his headquarters.

On December 23, 1642, several shepherds at Edgehill claimed to have witnessed a spectral reenactment of the entire skirmish. It began with the sound of distant drums which, as they got nearer, were joined by "the noise of soldiers giving out their last groans."

LEFT: The first major battle of the English Civil War took place at Edgehill, and has been refought several times since by two spectral armies.

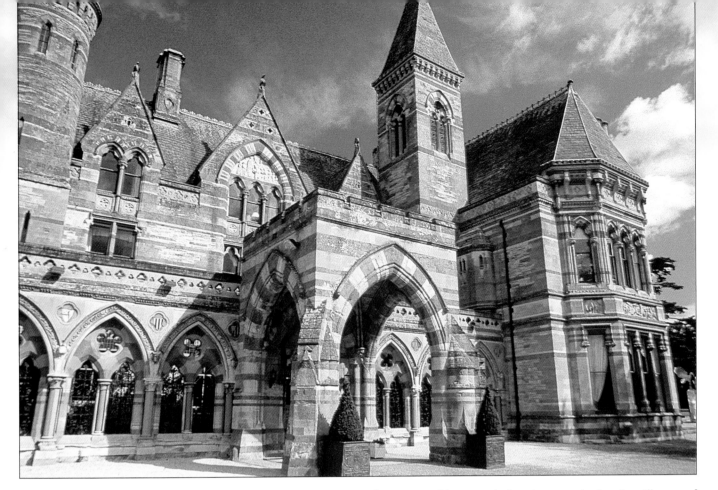

ABOVE: The Gothic appearance of Ettington Park Hotel makes it look every inch the haunted house of tradition.

There then appeared in the air "the same incorporeall souldiers that made those clamours," and a full-scale clash of phantom armies took place in the sky above the original battlefield. As the ethereal battle ended, the shepherds rushed to nearby Kineton village, where they repeated on oath before William Wood, a Justice of the Peace, and the Reverend Samuel Marshall, what they had witnessed. The phantom armies reappeared over several nights, and were witnessed on Christmas Day in "the same tumultuous and warlike manner, fighting with as much spite and spleen as formerly." When word reached the king in Oxford, he dispatched six men of "good repute and integrity" to investigate the sighting. They witnessed a reenactment of the dreadful battle and three of them, who had fought in the conflict, recognized several of the ghostly combatants.

Edgehill is said to occasionally echo with the spectral vestiges of the bloody skirmish. The hoofbeats of invisible cavalrymen have been heard thundering down roads in the dead of night, while the agonized screams of the wounded and dying are said to rend the air around what is still one of Warwickshire's most striking hillsides.

ETTINGTON PARK HOTEL
Ettington, Warwickshire

The Gothic appearance of this hotel, the oldest part of which dates back to the Tudor period, looks every inch the haunted house of tradition. It was for centuries the home of one of Warwickshire's oldest families, the Shirleys, and was used as a location for the 1963 film of Shirley Jackson's ghost story, *The Haunting of Hill House.*

As twilight dapples the old house in shadow, a "gray lady" has been known to materialize near the great stone staircase and drifts about the spot where she reputedly died after being pushed down the stairs. Another ghost, who staff have christened Lady Emma, sometimes glides along the terrace, her translucent figure in a flowing white dress. Meanwhile, on the banks of the River Stour, which flows through the grounds, the wraiths of two children wearing old-fashioned clothing have been seen. One guest was woken by the sound of a child sobbing outside, and on looking out of the window, saw the phantoms gazing pensively into the river. Finally, in the library bar, a copy of Sir Walter Scott's *St. Ronan's Well* used to be lifted off the shelf and flung across the room, where it always opened to a page which contains a curse.

"A MERRY PLACE ... IN DAYS OF YORE; BUT SOMETHING AILS IT NOW— THE PLACE IS CURSED."

THE CURSE ON THE PAGE OF *ST. RONAN'S WELL* AT ETTINGTON PARK HOTEL

BERKELEY CASTLE
Berkeley, Gloucestershire

Built in the 12th century and standing at the center of the picturesque Vale of Berkeley, this magnificent monument to a bygone age has remained in the possession of the same family for nearly eight hundred action-packed years. Visitors to the castle can still see a deep dungeon in the old keep, into which were once thrown the rotting carcasses of animals, accompanied every so often, it is said, by those of the lower classes who had offended the powerful Lord Berkeley. The stench from this disease-ridden pit provided an exquisitely horrific way to punish those of noble birth who had incurred the wrath of the Berkeley family—for nearby is a claustrophobic cell into which the unfortunate nobles were locked away, with only the stinking air from the nearby dungeon to breathe. Since few could survive long in the fetid atmosphere, it provided a convenient method by which to dispose of those who could not be seen to have actually been murdered.

It was in this living hell that Edward II was confined in 1327, following his deposal by his wife, Queen Isabella, and her lover, Roger Mortimer. It was their intention that a few days in the dreadful chamber would bring about the king's death. But his constitution surprised them. He became ill but recovered, and managed to survive five months before it was decided that a more direct approach was required— the queen instructed Edward's jailers, Sir John Maltravers and Sir Thomas Gurney, to dispose of her husband as they saw fit. Soon after, on September 21, 1327, Edward II suffered the most horrible death of any British monarch. He was seized and pinned face down on the bed, whereupon "a kind of horn or funnel was thrust into his fundament through which a red-hot spit was run up his bowels." Such was the king's agony that his screams are said to have been heard far beyond the castle walls, and have since echoed down the centuries on the anniversary of his death.

ABOVE: Edward II, who in 1327 suffered the most horrifying death of any English monarch.

OWLPEN MANOR
Owlpen, Gloucestershire

Set in a romantic valley in the heart of the Cotswolds, ensconced within a tall screen of leafy boughs and boasting a magnificent Tudor Great Hall, Owlpen Manor is possessed of an enchanting ambience that the march of time has done little to dispel. The de Olepenne family began its construction in 1450, and most of what is visible today had been completed by 1616, at which time the house had already acquired its most famous and oldest ghostly resident, Queen Margaret of Anjou.

The Queen was the formidable wife of the Lancastrian Henry VI, whose weak and ineffectual reign witnessed the most acute phase of the Wars of the Roses. Margaret joined forces with Richard Neville, known as "Warwick the Kingmaker," in an attempt to restore her husband to the throne of England, from which he had been deposed by the Yorkist Edward IV. On the night of May 3, 1471, she is said to have slept the night in the Tapestry Room at Owlpen Manor. Next day her son, Prince Edward, was killed as he fled the field after the Battle of Tewkesbury and headed for sanctuary at nearby Tewkesbury Abbey. It is said to be the shock of Edward's death that brings the Queen's sad specter back to haunt the rooms and corridors of the manor where she spent her last happy night, with her hopes of victory high.

During World War II, the owner of the house agreed to the billeting of several young evacuees, and on the morning after their arrival, the children asked the owner why she wasn't still wearing the "beautiful dress" they'd seen her wearing the previous evening. Since she had not seen the children the previous evening—and since she had certainly not been wearing such a dress—she asked them to describe it. Their descriptions tallied with the type of dress that a well-to-do medieval lady would have worn, and the owner was able to explain to the children that they had been welcomed by the manor's illustrious ghost!

PRESTBURY
Prestbury, Gloucestershire

❧❧❧❧❧❧❧❧❧❧❧❧❧❧❧❧

Prestbury vies with Pluckley in Kent for the title of "most haunted village in England." Its best-known spectral inhabitant is a hooded monk known as "The Black Abbot," who appears most often at Christmas and Easter and on All Souls' Day. His ghost seldom deviates from a route that begins inside the village church, crosses the churchyard and, having kept a straight trajectory through the grounds of the old priory, vanishes into the wall of a cottage on the High Street, where he announces his arrival by noisily moving things around in the attic. On November 22, 1990, Derek Stafford photographed the floodlit gravestones in the churchyard. Although he saw nothing at the time, he was astonished when—upon developing his pictures—he discovered a mysterious dark figure on one of the prints (see page 34).

Inevitably, the many skirmishes of the numerous conflicts to which this part of the country was privy, have contributed generously to the ghostly populace of the village. A spectral horseman on a galloping brilliant white "charger" has been known to visit Shaw Green Lane in the early hours of misty spring mornings. He is thought to be the ghost of a messenger who, in 1471, was passing through the village en route to Edward IV's camp at Tewkesbury, when he was shot dead by a Lancastrian archer. Interestingly, over the years, his phantom seems to be wasting away, since more recent sightings describe him as being little more than a dull glow.

The Burgage, the oldest street in the village, was billeted during the Civil War by a detachment of Parliamentarian soldiers. Each night they would string rope across the road as a security measure against Royalist forces. One night their trap yielded a rich dividend when a Royalist dispatch rider, heading to Gloucester from Sudeley Castle, galloped straight into the rope and was flung into the arms of his waiting captors, who executed him on the spot. Although the rider is never seen, his steed's hoofbeats are often heard in the dead of night, pounding along the Burgage until they stop abruptly when the phantom rider undergoes his ignoble fall, over and over again.

SNOWSHILL MANOR
Snowshill, Gloucestershire

❧❧❧❧❧❧❧❧❧❧❧❧❧❧❧❧❧❧

There is something slightly dark and mysterious about Snowshill Manor, located in one of the most timeless and remote villages in the Cotswolds. Once owned by Catherine Parr, the sixth and last wife of Henry VIII, it was bought in 1918

ABOVE: The sleepy ambience of Owlpen Manor is such that Queen Margaret of Anjou is still drawn to it almost 600 years after her death.

by Charles Paget Wade, who proceeded to restore the manor, and then fill it with what must surely be one of the the most extraordinary and eccentric collections of curios ever amassed beneath one residential roof. He gave the house to the National Trust in 1951, and visitors can now enjoy the fruits of one man's scholarly searches for the interesting. Each room is dedicated to a particular subject, and every conceivable quirk of fad and fashion from the past four hundred years is shown in rooms with names such as "Admiral," "Dragon," "Nadir," "Seraphim," and "Seventh Heaven" exquisitely painted above their doors. Guides working at the old house have often heard footsteps pacing across the floors of rooms that are known to be empty, and generally accept that the footsteps belong to Charles Wade's ghost, as he returns to check up on his unique collection.

MINSTER LOVELL HALL
Minster Lovell, Oxfordshire

❧❧❧❧❧❧❧❧❧❧❧❧❧❧❧❧❧❧❧❧❧❧❧

The ruins of Minster Lovell Hall are tucked away behind the delightful St. Kenelm's church on the tranquil banks of the River Windrush, in what is one of England's most beautiful villages. It is haunted by the ghost of Francis, the first Viscount Lovell, a fervent Yorkist who fled to the Continent following the defeat of his king, Richard III, at the Battle of Bosworth in August 1485. Francis then made his way to Ireland, where the pretender Lambert Simnel was crowned king and, in his company, returned to Yorkshire to raise an army, which met with the forces of Henry VII at the Battle of Stoke in June 1487. Defeated again, Francis is said to have escaped by swimming his horse across the River Trent and riding back to Minster Lovell Hall, where he had himself locked up in an underground room, the location of which was known only to an old retainer. With only his pet dog for company, Francis was dependent upon this faithful servant for food and drink. One day, the servant died suddenly, leaving his master incarcerated and helpless in what became his underground prison—and eventually his tomb. There Francis remained until the 18th century when, during the fitting of a new chimney, the builders uncovered a large underground vault in which they found the skeleton of a man sprawled across a table, with the bones of a little dog at its feet. Francis's doleful revenant has wandered the ruins ever since, a forlorn figure in a billowing cloak, often accompanied by the dreadful sounds of "groans, footsteps, and rustling papers" emanating from "somewhere beneath the ground."

THE ROLLRIGHT STONES
Long Compton, Oxfordshire

These mystical stones, standing upon a hill overlooking the village of Long Compton, are the source of a curious legend. The story goes that a king and his army set out to conquer the land, but when they arrived on the summit of the hill, the king met a witch, who told him:

> *Seven long strides shalt thou take,*
> *And if Long Compton then can'st see*
> *King of England thou shalt be.*

The king, safe in the knowledge that the exposed hilltop afforded an excellent view of the village beneath, sneered back:

> *Stick, stock, stone,*
> *As King of England I shall be known.*

Confidently, he took seven strides forward, only to find his view obstructed by a huge mound. Turning back to the chortling hag, he heard her chant:

> *As Long Compton thou can'st not see,*
> *King of England thou shalt not be!*
> *Rise up stick, stand still stone.*
>
> *For King of England thou shall be none,*
> *Thou and thy men hoarstones shall be*
> *And I myself an elder tree.*

And so the king met his fate, and the "King's Stone" can still be seen on the peaceful hillside above the village. Nearby stands a larger circle of between sixty and eighty stones, said to be the "Kings Army," which, it is claimed, can never be accurately counted, since no two attempts will ever yield the same total. On the edge of a nearby field stand five larger stones, huddled together in conspirational formation. They are known as the "Whispering Knights" and are said to have been five warriors who were plotting against the king when the spell fell upon them.

ST. JOHN'S COLLEGE
Oxford, Oxfordshire

Oxford, the "city of dreaming spires," can boast a veritable array of famous names that return in spectral form to its college cloisters and ancient buildings. But none have chosen to do so in quite as dramatic a fashion as the ghost of Archbishop William Laud (1573–1645), who haunts various locations around St. John's College.

Having studied at St. John's, William Laud became president of the college in 1611, before leaving it for an ecclesiastical career. He returned in 1629 to take up his position as Chancellor of Oxford University and then, in 1633, became the Archbishop of Canterbury. This led to Laud becoming embroiled in the political and religious arguments that would eventually result in the English Civil War. Laud was a fervent believer in, and a strong exponent of, Royal power and High Church ritual, which led to his indictment for treason by a vengeful Parliament in 1644. Laud's illustrious career ended when he was beheaded in London in 1645, although it was eighteen years before his body was returned to Oxford and buried in the chapel at St. John's College.

Laud certainly does not sleep peacefully in its hallowed earth, for many is the time that his somber ghost has been seen around the quad and grounds of his old college. Many witnesses have hardly paid him a second glance when he appears before them. It is only when he suddenly lifts his head off his shoulders and bowls the leering lump of bone and gristle along the ground toward them, that they either turn heel and run, or else faint.

ABOVE: The ghost of Archbishop Laud makes uniquely disturbing appearances at St. John's College, Oxford.

OPPOSITE: On an Oxfordshire hillside, a petrified army stands frozen in time, turned to stone by a witch.

CAPITAL TERRORS
and HOME COUNTY
HORRORS

The City is of Night, but not of Sleep;
    There sweet sleep is not for the weary
        brain;
The pitiless hours like years and ages
    creep,
    A night seems termless hell. This
        dreadful strain
Of thought and consciousness which never
    ceases,
    Or which some moments' stupor but
        increases,
This, worse than woe, makes wretches
    there insane.

FROM *THE CITY OF DREADFUL NIGHT*
BY JAMES THOMSON ("B.V.")

LONDON, BERKSHIRE, BUCKINGHAMSHIRE, BEDFORDSHIRE, & HERTFORDSHIRE

ondon is reputed to be the most haunted capital city in the world, with ghosts that span centuries and provide glimpses of a dark and sinister past. To the city's north and west stretch the counties of Hertfordshire, Bedfordshire, Berkshire, and Buckinghamshire, all of which are steeped in folklore and legend. Satan and his devilish cohorts seem to have been much in evidence throughout the Middle Ages, and several peculiarities across the landscape have long been attributed to demonic interference. On the other hand, religious fervor has been a marked characteristic of many of the inhabitants, and the likes of John Bunyan are indelibly linked with the area, with several of the settings from *The Pilgrim's Progress* still identifiable around the countryside. All in all, it is an enchanting landscape against which all manner of hauntings have evolved.

KEY

1. Highgate Cemetery
2. St Botolph's Church
3. The Tower of London
4. The Great Bed of Ware
5. Bisham Abbey
6. The Ostrich Inn
7. The Royal Stag
8. Claydon House
9. St Mary the Virgin
10. Minsden Chapel
11. St Peter's Church

HIGHGATE CEMETERY
Highgate, London

Sprawled across twenty grassy hillside acres, and opened in 1839, Highgate Cemetery quickly became the most sought-after resting place in London, and fashion-conscious Victorians wouldn't be seen dead in any other burial ground. By the dawn

PREVIOUS PAGES: The awe-inspiring bulk of the Tower of London, possibly the most haunted building in Britain.

OPPOSITE: Do vampires roam the tangled pathways that snake through Highgate Cemetery?

of the 20th century, thousands of people had been laid to rest in its hallowed ground, among them many famous and illustrious names. The monuments to the dead became ever more ambitious, as families desperately struggled to outdo one another by providing yet more ostentatious resting places for their loved ones. But as the dark days of World War II descended upon the capital, the cemetery's fortunes saw a severe downturn, and by the 1960s the once proud necropolis had been abandoned. Decay and neglect crept unchecked among the tombs, as the roots of ever-advancing vegetation split apart the magnificent graves and left their twisted masonry sprawled across toppled columns.

Rumors were soon circulating of sinister cults holding strange ceremonies after dark in the abandoned ruins. The local newspaper, the *Hampstead and Highgate Express*, began to

ABOVE: An angelic figure's sorrowful expression seems to reflect the sad decline of Highgate Cemetery, Victorian London's most ambitious necropolis.

from the bells in the old, disused chapel.

A massive restoration project, started in the 1980s by the enthusiastic Friends of Highgate Cemetery, went some way to reversing the neglect of the previous decades. As they cleared the pathways and uncovered many of the spectacular tombs, the ghostly activity began to recede. Today, spectral sightings are reduced to the ghost of a mad old woman, whose long gray hair streams behind her as she races among the graves, searching for her children, whom she is supposed to have murdered in a fit of insane rage; and a shrouded figure who gazes pensively into space, seemingly oblivious to the presence of witnesses unless they get too close—whereupon it vanishes, only to reappear a short distance away, adopting the same meditative pose.

ST. BOTOLPH'S CHURCH
Bishopsgate, London

In 1982, photographer Chris Brackley took a picture inside this historic old church. At the time, the only people present were himself and his wife. When the photograph was developed, he was astonished to note that a figure in old-fashioned garb was standing on the balcony to the right of the altar. The negative was subjected to considerable expert analysis, which revealed that that there was no double exposure to the film. Nor was any of Chris's equipment faulty. The only explanation for the mysterious figure was that someone must actually have been standing on the balcony when the picture was taken. A few years later, Chris was contacted by a builder who had been employed to do restoration work in St. Botolph's crypt. He explained that, in knocking down a wall, he had inadvertently disturbed a pile of old coffins. One had come open to reveal a reasonably well-preserved body, the face of which bore an uncanny resemblance to the figure that had appeared in Chris's photograph.

receive letters from frightened readers telling of ghostly encounters around the cemetery. One man, whose car had broken down on the road outside, was terrified by a hideous apparition with glowing red eyes that glared at him through the rusting, iron gates. Another man, walking along the darkly forbidding Swain's Lane, found himself suddenly knocked to the ground by a fearsome creature that "seemed to glide" from the wall of the cemetery. He was only saved by the headlights of an approaching car that caused the "thing" to dissolve into thin air. When it was subsequently suggested that a vampire might be loose in the old cemetery, a veritable barrage of journalists, camera crews, eager occultists, and the "just plain curious" swarmed around the decaying and grim mausoleums, garlic and crucifixes at the ready, and the hunt for the undead was under way.

Meanwhile, more letters telling of frightening encounters in the vicinity of Swain's Lane continued to grace the pages of the local press. A ghostly cyclist seen puffing his way up the steep incline had scared the life out of a young mother, while other unfortunate locals had witnessed a tall man in a top hat, who would walk nonchalantly across the road and then disappear into the cemetery wall. His nebulous stroll was always, the witnesses reported, accompanied by a mournful tolling

RIGHT: A ghostly figure (detail above) made an uninvited appearance in this photograph of St. Botolph's Church.

THE TOWER OF LONDON
London

❧ ❧ ❧ ❧ ❧ ❧ ❧ ❧ ❧ ❧ ❧ ❧ ❧ ❧

Grim, gray, and awe-inspiring, the Tower of London has dominated the city landscape and the pages of history since its construction by William the Conqueror in 1078. Today it is, perhaps, the most haunted building in England.

The Wakefield Tower is haunted by that most tragic of English monarchs, Henry VI, whose weak and ineffectual reign ended here with his murder "in the hour before midnight" on May 21, 1471, as he knelt at prayer. Tradition asserts that the knife with which he was "stikk'd full of deadly holes" was wielded by the Duke of Gloucester (later the infamous Richard III). On the anniversary of his murder, Henry's mournful wraith is said to appear as the clock ticks toward midnight, and to fitfully pace around the interior of the Wakefield Tower until, upon the last stroke of midnight, he fades slowly into the stone and rests peacefully for another year.

The massive White Tower is the oldest and most forbidding of all the Tower of London's buildings, and its winding stone corridors are the eerie haunt of a "white lady" who was once seen standing at a window, waving to a group of children in the building opposite. It may well be her "cheap perfume" that impregnates the air around the entrance to St. John's Chapel, and which has caused many a guard to retch upon inhaling its pungent aroma.

In the gallery where Henry VIII's impressive and exaggerated suit of armour is exhibited, several guards have spoken of a terrible crushing sensation that suddenly descends upon them as they enter, but which lifts the moment they stagger, shaking, from the room. A guard who was patrolling through here one stormy night got the sudden and unnerving sensation that someone had thrown a heavy cloak over him. As he struggled to free himself, the garment was seized from behind and pulled tight around his throat by his phantom attacker. Managing to break free from its sinister grasp,

ABOVE: The names of those who were taken as prisoners into the Tower of London through Traitors' Gate read like a *Who's Who* of English history.

he rushed back to the guardroom, where the marks upon his neck bore vivid testimony to his brush with the unseen assailant.

A memorial on Tower Green remembers all the unfortunate souls who have been executed here over the centuries. Anne Boleyn and Lady Jane Grey are both said to appear in the vicinity, while the ghost of Margaret Pole, Countess of Salisbury, returns here in a dramatic and alarming fashion. At the age of seventy-two she, became an unwitting and undeserving target for Henry VIII's petty vengeance. Her son,

Cardinal Pole, had vilified the king's claim to be head of the Church of England. But since Cardinal Pole was safely ensconced in France, Henry had his mother brought to the block on May 27, 1541. When told by the executioner to kneel, the spirited old lady refused. "So should traitors do, and I am none," she sneered. The executioner raised his axe, took a swing at her, and then chased the countess around the scaffold, where he hacked her to death. The spectacle has been repeated several times on the anniversary of her death, as her screaming phantom continues to be chased throughout eternity by a ghostly executioner.

The Bloody Tower, the very name of which conjures up all manner of gruesome images, is home to the most poignant shades that drift through this fearful fortress, the "Princes in the Tower." When Edward IV died suddenly in April 1483, his twelve-year-old son was destined to succeed him as Edward V. However, before his coronation could take place, Edward and his younger brother, Richard, were declared illegitimate by Parliament, and their uncle, the Duke of Gloucester, instead ascended the throne as Richard III. The boys, meanwhile, had been sent to the Tower of London, ostensibly in preparation for Edward's coronation, and were often seen happily playing around the grounds. But by the autumn of 1483, they vanished and were never seen again. It was always assumed that they had been murdered on Richard's instructions, and that their bodies were buried somewhere within the grounds of the Tower. When two skeletons were uncovered beneath a staircase of the White Tower in 1674, they were presumed to be the remains of the two

ABOVE: The little Princes, Edward and Richard, whose disappearance from the Tower of London in 1483 created one of history's greatest mysteries and London's most poignant hauntings.

little princes, and were afforded a Royal burial in Westminster Abbey. The whimpering wraiths of the two children, dressed in white nightgowns and clutching each other in terror, have frequently been seen in the dimly lit rooms of their prison. Witnesses are moved to pity, and long to reach out and console the pathetic specters. But should they do so, the trembling revenants back slowly against the wall and fade into the fabric.

Returning to the White Tower and the fearless custody guards who wander its interior in the dead of night, there is the occasion when Mr. Arthur Crick decided to take a rest as he made his rounds. Sitting on a ledge, he slipped off his right shoe, and was in the process of massaging his tired foot when an eerie voice behind him whispered, "There's only you and I here." This elicited from Arthur the earthly response: "Just let me get this bloody shoe on, and there'll only be you!"

THE GREAT BED OF WARE
V & A Museum, London

This impressive bed, measuring an incredible 133 inches long by 130½ inches wide, is reputedly the most haunted bed in Britain. It was supposedly made for King Edward IV in 1463 by carpenter Jonas Fosbrooke, and was intended for the sole use of the monarch. When Edward's son, Edward V, became one of the tragic "Princes in the Tower," the bed was sold and passed through the bedrooms of a succession of inns in Ware,

Hertfordshire. Once, in the 17th century, twelve married couples are reputed to have shared the bed during a festival when there was, literally, no room at the inn! But the delightfully stuffy spirit of Fosbrooke did not take kindly to riffraff enjoying the luxury of his creation. He would disturb the sleep of anyone who dared sleep in it by pinching and scratching them in a most malicious and unpleasant manner. Indeed, so well known were his spectral attacks that it was customary for guests at the various inns to drink a toast to the bed and the ghost before retiring for the night.

BISHAM ABBEY
Bisham, Berkshire
✿ ✿

ABOVE: Though it probably dates from a later century, legend has made the Great Bed of Ware the creation of a 15th-century Royal carpenter, and imbued it with a truly sinister reputation.

Bisham Abbey and its grounds are now home to the England's National Sports Center and are used, among other things, as a training ground by the English football squad—who would, no doubt, greatly benefit from the managerial skills of the resident ghost. The ghost is thought to be that of Dame Elizabeth Hoby, whose somber effigy can still be seen at nearby All Saints church. In life, this lady was a brilliant scholar, fluent in Greek and Latin, and an enthusiastic composer of religious treatises. She had high hopes for her son, William. But the boy lacked any enthusiasm for studying and, worse still, turned out to be a poor scholar with little aptitude for the languages in which his

mother excelled. He would often blot his copybooks and send his tyrannical mother into fits of incandescent rage, during which she would mercilessly beat the poor boy. One day, following a particularly poor learning session, young William Hoby's slovenly behavior pushed his mother's self-control to

RIGHT: Bisham Abbey, and the land where the abbey once stood, is the haunt of Dame Elizabeth Hoby, who suffers eternal remorse for the murder of her son.

ABOVE: Spirits of a decidedly sinister nature frequent The Ostrich Inn at Colnbrook, thanks to the nefarious exploits of a 14th-century landlord named Jarman.

the limit and, in order to teach him a firm lesson, she administered a severe beating and then locked him in a dark closet. Unfortunately, she was then summoned to London by Queen Elizabeth I and, before she left, forgot to tell the servants of William's whereabouts. By the time she returned, the boy had starved to death, and Dame Elizabeth's eternal fate was sealed.

She died in 1609, a penitent and wretched old lady, and her ghost has walked the abbey and grounds ever since. Ponderous footsteps have been heard shuffling along corridors at night, and these are occasionally accompanied by the sound of remorseful weeping. But most alarming of all must be the appearance of her mournful wraith, which has been described as resembling a photographic negative because of its black face and hands and white dress. She glides around the building, eternally washing blood from her hands in a basin of water that floats in front of her "without visible means of support"!

THE OSTRICH INN
Colnbrook, Berkshire
❀❀❀❀❀❀❀❀❀❀❀❀❀❀❀❀❀❀❀❀

This old, atmospheric inn is located in the ancient village of Colnbrook, and was once an important stopover on the main stagecoach route that ran from London to Bath. Not wishing to enter the fracas of the endless battle to proclaim itself the oldest pub in England, The Ostrich plays it safe and claims to be the "fourth oldest," based on records of the inn that date as far back as 1165. One thing it can certainly claim,

however, is that it was the first pub in England to ever be featured in a novel, based on its mention in *Thomas of Reading*, which was written in the late 16th century by Thomas Deloney.

It was Deloney's reporting of the nefarious exploits of a former landlord called Jarman that secured The Ostrich's place in Berkshire legend. His infamous crimes are generally thought to have taken place some time around the 1300s. In those days, wealthy travelers would pause at the inn to change from their mud-spattered clothes into the finery expected for their appearances before the monarch at nearby Windsor Castle. Many of these wayfarers would carry vast sums of money with them, a fact that didn't go unnoticed by Jarman, who had soon devised a profitable and intricate method of relieving them of both their riches and their lives.

Whenever seemingly affluent patrons arrived at his inn, Jarman would waste no time in plying them with strong drink. Having arranged for the strangers to sleep in his "best room," he would give them time to collapse into bed. Once Jarman was sure that the guests were fast asleep, he would undo two bolts on the ceiling in the room beneath. This would cause their bed to tilt downward at a 45-degree angle, sending the insensible sleepers tumbling into a vat of boiling fat that Jarman always kept ready in the room below. He would then steal the guests' belongings, sell their horses and clothes to the unquestioning gypsies, and dispose of the bodies into the nearby river.

BELOW: Whenever the ghostly handprint appears on this glass pane at The Royal Stag, staff are reminded of the unfortunate child who froze to death outside the window in the 19th century.

Jarman seems to have profited immensely from his activities, and to have escaped any suspicion for many years. But then one night, a suitably drunk stranger had crawled into the bed when the amount of alcohol he had consumed forced him to climb straight back out and make use of the room's chamber pot. As he answered the call of nature, he was astonished to see the head of his bed suddenly tilt and disappear into the floor. His terrified shouts roused the other guests, and Jarman's murderous career was over. On the gallows, Jarman boasted of having killed more than sixty people, although the actual total is believed to be closer to fifteen.

Staff at the inn, where a decidedly old-world charm still holds sway, are often troubled by the "sinister atmosphere" that seems to hang over certain sections, and several landlords have complained of their nightly repose being rudely disturbed by the eerie sound of creaking boards, ghostly sighs, and spectral bumps, which are attributed to one of Jarman's long-ago victims.

THE ROYAL STAG
Datchet, Berkshire

✿ ✿ ✿ ✿ ✿ ✿ ✿ ✿ ✿ ✿ ✿

This picturesque pub, which stands on a corner next to the parish church in the village of Datchet, is the perfect place in which to while away a cold winter's afternoon. Such is its timeless feel, that hours can pass by and seem like only moments—a fact that, on one long-ago occasion, led to a tragedy that has resulted in one of England's most bizarre pub hauntings. In a bleak and snow-covered midwinter, reportedly some time during the Victorian age, a laborer and his young son arrived at the door of The Royal Stag. Being a responsible parent, the man sent the boy to play in the churchyard next door, while he settled down to enjoy the hospitality afforded by the atmospheric hostelry. The child amused himself in the snow for a time, but then the cold began to chill his bones and, walking to the window of the pub that still faces onto the little churchyard, he attempted to attract his father's attention. The man, however, was having too much of a good time to pay any heed to his son's plight, and pointedly ignored his offspring. In a last

desperate attempt to lure his father from his pint, the boy pressed his hand hard against the windowpane, and then sank into the snow, where he froze to death. Ever since that tragic day, his ghostly handprint has made frequent appearances upon the pane. Sometimes it is visible for months on end, other times its pathetic imprint is there for but a few hours. When it appeared in 1979, a national newspaper removed the panel and subjected it to scientific analysis. The results proved that it was just an ordinary piece of very old glass, and the technicians could detect nothing else. Meanwhile, the ghostly imprint had made a mysterious appearance on the pane of modern glass fitted in its place. A photograph, taken when the hand manifested in February 2000, is reproduced opposite.

ABOVE: Sir Edmund Verney, whose hand remained clasped around the Royal standard at the battle of Edgehill, despite attempts by Cromwell's troops to prise it off.

CLAYDON HOUSE
Middle Claydon, Buckinghamshire

✿ ✿ ✿ ✿ ✿ ✿ ✿ ✿ ✿ ✿ ✿

The ghost of a former owner, Sir Edmund Verney, Royalist standard-bearer at the battle of Edgehill in 1642 (see page 38), is said to haunt this house. Sir Edmund was captured by Cromwell's troops and ordered to surrender the Colors. This he refused to do, saying, "My life is my own but my standard is the King's." The soldiers killed Sir Edmund— but when they attempted to seize the standard, they found that his fingers could not be prised from around it, and so were forced to hack off his hand. The Royalists recaptured the banner and found the hand still clasped around it. Sir Edmund's body was never recovered, but his hand, with its identifying signet ring, was sent back to Claydon, where it was interred. Sir Edmund's ghost has haunted the building ever since. His tormented wraith, in 17th-century costume, has been seen fitfully pacing along corridors, or standing dolefully on the stairs, a look of dismay upon his face as he searches to find the hand that he lost for loyalty to his king.

"MY LIFE IS MY OWN, BUT MY STANDARD IS THE KING'S."

SIR EDMUND VERNEY, SACRIFICING HIS LIFE FOR CHARLES I

St. Mary the Virgin
Marston Moretaine, Bedfordshire

❦❦❦❦❦❦❦❦❦❦❦❦❦❦❦❦❦❦❦❦❦

This pretty church was virtually rebuilt in 1445 and contains several intriguing carved timbers as well as screen paintings. It also possesses a massive west tower that is set curiously apart from the rest of the building. In reality, this unique feature was probably intended as a refuge from flooding, since the church stands in a low-lying valley. But local lore has attributed its detachment to the devil, who is said to have pitched up at the church one night, intent on stealing the tower, but found it far too heavy and abandoned it after a few short steps.

ABOVE: The devil was renowned for stealing entire churches from medieval England.

LEFT: T.W. Latchmore reputedly photographed a ghostly monk among the tottering ruins of Hertfordshire's Minsden Chapel in 1907.

Minsden Chapel
Near Hitchin, Hertfordshire

❦❦❦❦❦❦❦❦❦❦❦❦❦❦❦❦❦❦❦❦❦

Hidden from view by a wooded copse, and reached by a brisk walk along a muddy bridle path, the crumbling remnants of Minsden Chapel have tottered on the edge of ruin for at least three hundred years. Built in the 14th century as a chapel of ease for pilgrims en route to St. Albans Abbey, it had fallen into disrepair by the 18th century, when its secluded woodland setting made it a favored and romantic location for weddings. Unfortunately, as Mary Horn was plighting her troth to Enoch West in 1738, a lump of masonry suddenly dislodged itself from the roof and fell earthward, knocking the prayer book from the priest's hand. The powers that be decided that enough was enough, and the chapel was abandoned. It has remained little more than a melancholic ruin ever since. In the early 20th century it became indelibly linked with the Hertfordshire historian, Reginald Hine, whose fondness for what was left of the chapel led to his leasing it from the church for his lifetime. He issued a dire warning to "trespassers and sacrilegious persons" that he would "proceed against them with the utmost rigor of the law and after my death and burial, I will endeavor in all ghostly ways to protect and haunt its hallowed walls." Following his death in 1949 he was buried here, and his cracked tombstone now rests beneath a lush carpet of weed and nettle. Unsurprisingly, the crumbling edifice is haunted, its ghost being that of a phantom monk who appears on Halloween at midnight and ascends a long-vanished flight of stairs at the chapel's northeast corner. The monk's appearance is always preceded by a mysterious tolling of Minsden's lost bells, and his passage is marked by the eerie, though solemn, sound of plaintive music. In 1907, photographer T. W. Latchmore took a photograph of the ruins and claimed to have captured the spectral monk on film. The picture is wonderfully atmospheric, and is reproduced opposite for you to decide whether it is genuine or just a clever fake.

BELOW: The tomb of Anne Grimston, who refused to repent on her deathbed, sneering that if there is an afterlife, "seven trees will render asunder my tomb."

ST. PETER'S CHURCH
Tewin, Hertfordshire

Perched on a slight incline, this squat church of flint and brick is not overly impressive. It is ringed by a peaceful churchyard, where rests the body of a heretic whose grave is surrounded by a wrought-iron fence, and whose heresy is remembered by the bizarre fulfillment of a deathbed prophesy. The heretic's name was Lady Anne Grimston. She was, in life, said to have been a Sadducean and, therefore, did not believe in the Resurrection of the Dead. As she lay dying in November 1780, she ignored the vicar's entreaties to recant her heresy, and refused to allow him to administer the last rites. "If, indeed, there is life hereafter," she is said to have sneered, "trees will render asunder my tomb."

Lady Anne's body was laid to rest in St. Peter's churchyard where, either by the hand of fate or by the machinations of an opportunist clergyman, several trees have indeed sprouted through her tomb, lifting it slightly and depositing great chunks of moss-clad masonry onto the carpet of nettle and bramble beneath which her mortal remains now lie.

SPECTRAL SHIPS, HISTORIC HILLS, and ENGLAND'S MOST HAUNTED VILLAGE

The land's sharp features seemed to be
The Century's corpse outleant,
His crypt the cloudy canopy,
The wind his death-lament.
The ancient pulse of germ and birth
Was shrunken hard and dry,
And every spirit upon earth
Seemed fervorless as I.

FROM *THE DARKLING THRUSH*
BY THOMAS HARDY

SURREY, WEST SUSSEX, EAST SUSSEX, & KENT

The counties of Kent, Surrey, and East and West Sussex are rich in history, lore, and legend. The coastal areas have long provided a gateway through which conquering invaders—Romans, Saxons, and Jutes—have passed. In 1066, William Duke of Normandy led the last successful invasion of England, defeating King Harold at Senlac Ridge in the Battle of Hastings. Over a century later, on a tranquil meadow in Surrey, King John sealed the Magna Carta and laid one of the most important foundations of English law. But these momentous events would also be enshrined in legend. Ghostly soldiers became a firm ethereal fixture of the landscape and, such was the hatred of King John, that for years after his death, his spirit was said to roam the Surrey countryside in the shape of a monstrous werewolf!

The despotic actions of Henry VIII made a sizable contribution to the spectral populace, with three of his wives haunting Hampton Court Palace. In the 20th century, a tiny Kentish village called Pluckley achieved universal fame as the most haunted village in England.

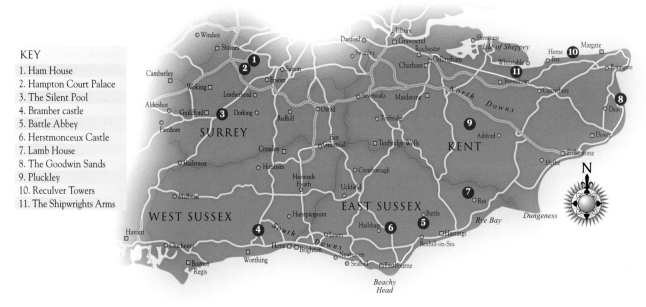

KEY
1. Ham House
2. Hampton Court Palace
3. The Silent Pool
4. Bramber castle
5. Battle Abbey
6. Herstmonceux Castle
7. Lamb House
8. The Goodwin Sands
9. Pluckley
10. Reculver Towers
11. The Shipwrights Arms

HAM HOUSE
Petersham, Surrey

✖ ✖ ✖ ✖ ✖ ✖ ✖ ✖ ✖ ✖ ✖ ✖ ✖ ✖ ✖ ✖ ✖ ✖ ✖ ✖

Known as the "sleeping beauty of country houses," this splendid building has changed little since the 17th century. Built in 1610 as a modest country residence by Sir Thomas Vavasour, the house was acquired in 1637 by William Murray, first Earl of Dysart, who, as a youth, had enjoyed the "enviable"

PREVIOUS PAGES: A ghostly ship is often seen heading for the treacherous reaches of Kent's Goodwin Sands.

position of whipping boy to the future Charles I. Chief among his duties was that he should be punished for the Prince's misbehavior! In 1651 he bequeathed the house to his daughter, Elizabeth Murray, Countess of Dysart and wife of Sir Lyonel Tollemache, by whom she had eleven children. Rumors were rife that she was also the mistress of Oliver Cromwell who, gossip maintained, was the father of her second son, Thomas. With the Restoration of the monarchy, Elizabeth became the lover of the Duke of Lauderdale, subsequently marrying him in 1672 following the death of Sir Lyonel.

An intriguing tale tells of the six-year-old daughter of a 19th-century butler at Ham House, who was invited by the

then owners, the ladies Tollemache, to stay at the property. In the early hours of the morning, the girl awoke to find a little old lady scratching with her fingers upon the wall by the fireplace. Sitting up to get a better view of the stranger, she seemed to disturb the woman, who came to the foot of the bed and proceeded to stare at the child with a fixed and horrible gaze. This sent the child into screaming hysterics, which in turn alerted other members of the household, who came racing to the room. They could find no sign of the old woman, but on searching the wall, they uncovered a secret compartment in which were papers that proved Elizabeth, the Countess of Dysart, had murdered her first husband in order to marry the Duke of Lauderdale.

HAMPTON COURT PALACE
Hampton Court, Surrey

In 1525, Cardinal Wolsey constructed a magnificent palace on the banks of the Thames. He lived in the completed building in regal splendor and entertained on such a lavish scale that his hospitality became the talk of Europe. But when he failed

ABOVE: Ham House, the "sleeping beauty of country houses," where the ghost of Oliver Cromwell's mistress proved that she had murdered her first husband.

in his attempts to persuade the Pope to annul the marriage of Henry VIII and Catherine of Aragon, his fate and downfall were sealed. In a last desperate attempt to buy his way back into Royal favor, the crestfallen Cardinal presented his "jewel on the Thames" to Henry, who gratefully accepted the gift and then promptly summoned Wolsey to answer charges of treason. Frail in both mind and body, the dejected cleric headed south from his see at York, but died en route at Leicester, wishing that he had "served God as diligently as I have served my King."

Henry wasted no time in introducing his second wife, Anne Boleyn, for whom he had divorced Catherine of Aragon, to the splendors of Wolsey's palace. Following her beheading due to alleged infidelities in 1536—although it is more likely that she was disposed of for failing to produce a male heir—her ghost has remained behind to drift forlornly through its passages and chambers wearing a blue dress. Henry was already courting Jane Seymour while Anne was still alive. When Jane became his third wife, however, she appears to have brought the despotic tyrant genuine contentment and provided him with his longed-for son and heir, Edward, born on October 12, 1537. Sadly, shortly afterward, Jane Seymour died from natural causes—and ever since, her phantom has made an annual pilgrimage to the palace on the anniversary of her son's birth. Holding an unflickering candle and with her head bent in sorrow, she glides eerily along corridors, passes through closed doors, and has, on occasion, shocked palace staff members so much that they have subsequently handed in their resignation.

But it is Henry's fifth wife, Catherine Howard, who makes the most dramatic return to Hampton Court Palace. Although she was still a mere teenager when she married the king in 1540, Catherine was certainly sexually experienced. Her past liaisons had included her music master, Henry Mannock, and a youthful nobleman named Dereham. She found the king physically repulsive, and sought solace in the arms of a young man at court, Thomas Culpeper. Servants' tittle-tattle brought her previous indiscretions to light, and not long afterward her adultery was exposed. Henry was furious at the betrayal. The unfortunate Culpeper soon languished in the Tower of London and was subsequently executed, as were Mannock and Dereham. The unfaithful queen found herself imprisoned in her chambers at Hampton Court. Brooding on her inevitable fate, Catherine decided that her only hope lay in meeting with her husband and pleading with him to spare her life. On November 4, 1541, knowing that Henry would be at prayer in the chapel, she broke free from her guards and ran through what is now known as the "Haunted Gallery," where she threw herself at the chapel's locked door, screaming at her husband to grant her an audience. The king listened in stony silence, and moments later the guards recaptured the hysterical girl and dragged her back to her chambers. On February 13, 1542, at

ABOVE: The ghost of Jane Seymour, Henry VIII's third wife, roams the corridors of Hampton Court Palace, carrying a candle.

RIGHT: The stone lions at Hampton Court have witnessed many Royal hauntings.

just twenty years of age, Catherine Howard went bravely to the block: "I die a Queen, but I had rather died the simple wife of Tom Culpeper. May God have mercy on my soul. Pray for me." She was smiling when the axe fell. Ever since, servants, noblemen, and, more recently, wardens have reported seeing her ghost, dressed in a white gown and racing toward the chapel, her face contorted into a terrifying, unearthly scream. Many visitors have reported a peculiar, icy coldness and an intense feeling of desperate sadness around the doors of the chapel itself, and some people have even witnessed a disembodied, ringed hand knocking upon the door. As recently as 1999, two women on separate guided tours fainted at exactly the same spot in the Haunted Gallery. Both women reported a sudden chill and said they felt as if they had been punched shortly before losing consciousness.

Hampton Court has more than thirty ghosts residing within its ancient fabric. History certainly does come alive here, and to explore its fascinating rooms and passages is to walk with kings and queens, lords and ladies, the famous and forgotten.

THE SILENT POOL
Near Shere, Surrey

A strange and uncanny stillness hangs over this sinister little lake, which ripples in a lonely setting near Shere, under the North Downs. In the 13th century, this whole area was dense forest, and legend holds that one day a stranger, dressed in rich apparel, arrived at the home of a poor woodcutter who lived nearby. The man was a widower, and his home was little more than a hovel that he shared with his young son and beautiful teenage daughter. But despite his poverty, the woodcutter invited the stranger to partake of whatever hospitality he could offer. As the noble visitor refreshed himself, the woodcutter's

ABOVE: An aura of melancholy still exudes from the Silent Pool, where a woodcutter's children were reputedly drowned through the evil actions of King John.

daughter went out to bathe in the pool. It was a warm day and she was enjoying an invigorating swim when she heard someone crashing through the undergrowth. She headed for the bank, but before she could reach dry land the stranger sped out of the forest and reared his horse over her clothing. The girl dived back into the water, and the stranger spurred his horse into the lake after her. The girl was a poor swimmer and was soon floundering in the deepest part of the pool, where her distress greatly amused the stranger, who continued toward her. At that moment her brother, having heard his sister's cries, raced to the pool and flung himself in to assist. But he, too, was a poor swimmer and, moments later, they had both slipped beneath the surface and drowned. Unmoved by their plight, the man rode from the water and galloped away.

A little while later, the woodcutter came to the pool in search of his children. Spotting their lifeless bodies floating on the surface, the grief-stricken man pulled them from the water and laid them upon the banks. It was then that he noticed a feather from the stranger's hat caught upon a tree, and realized what had happened. Vowing vengeance, he wandered the district intent on discovering the murderer's identity. He soon found out that the noble stranger had been none other than Prince John, Regent of England while his brother, Richard, was away fighting the Crusades.

Through the machinations of one of John's many enemies, the woodcutter secured an audience with the Regent at Guildford Castle. John failed to recognize the woodcutter and, having apparently forgotten his wickedness, expressed outrage at the murder of the children, declaring that the man responsible was to be punished. At this point the woodcutter threw down the feather and denounced John for the villain he was. Sadly, the legend does not reveal how the audience finished—but tradition states that it was the fate of the woodcutter's children that determined the barons in their resolve to confront John and force him into the sealing of the Magna Carta on Runnymede in 1215.

The long-ago tragedy is also believed to account for the peculiar and uncanny silence that often seems to emanate from the ominous pool, where the wraith of the murdered girl is, on occasion, said to drift beneath its rippling, sullen waters.

BRAMBER CASTLE
Bramber, West Sussex

❧❧❧❧❧❧❧❧❧❧❧❧❧❧❧❧❧❧❧❧❧

Only a 76-foot high fragment of the Norman castle wall, which stands upon a huge natural mound, now survives of what was once a proud and imposing fortress. In the reign of King John, the castle was owned by William de Braose, whose lavish lifestyle earned him the envy of the monarch—but whose involvement in the events that led to the sealing of the Magna Carta in 1215 incurred the king's displeasure. Determined to make an example of de Braose, the scheming sovereign commanded that the powerful baron surrender his four young children to be held as hostages against their father's future good behavior. When the preposterous demand met with a stubborn refusal, John sent an army to Bramber with instructions to take the children by force. Learning of the plan, de Braose gathered his family and fled to Ireland, where they were captured, returned to England, and imprisoned at Windsor Castle. There, the vengeful monarch had the children starved to death as a warning to the other rebellious barons that he, John, was not a man to be trifled with. Although they died at Windsor Castle, it is to the melancholic ruin of Bramber Castle that the pathetic wraiths of the murdered children return, Christmas being their favored time. The ragged, hollow-eyed wraiths of two girls and a boy wander the crumbling vestiges of their old home, their emaciated hands held out as if begging for food from witnesses, who are almost moved to tears by the sad and tragic apparitions.

BATTLE ABBEY
Battle, East Sussex

❧❧❧❧❧❧❧❧❧❧❧❧❧❧❧❧❧❧❧❧❧

In 1051, Edward the Confessor named William, Duke of Normandy as his heir to the English throne. But following Edward's death in January 1066, Harold Godwinson had himself crowned King of England. Furious at the betrayal, William planned an invasion and, in September 1066, he set sail for England, where he landed at Pevensey Bay. Harold was in the north of England, having just won a great victory over Viking invaders at Stamford Bridge. He hurried south, intent on seeing off William's claim to the throne; on October 13, 1066, his army arrived on Caldbec Hill, northwest of Hastings.

> **"IF WE WIN, AND GOD SEND WE MAY, I WILL FOUND AN ABBEY HERE FOR THE SALVATION OF THE SOULS OF ALL WHO FALL IN THE BATTLE."**
> WILLIAM THE CONQUEROR'S REPUTED PROMISE ON THE EVE OF THE BATTLE OF HASTINGS

The following morning the Saxon defenders moved onto nearby Senlac Ridge, confronting the Norman invaders who were positioned along its lower slope, and the Battle of

BELOW: The bloodstained specter of King Harold haunts the ruins of Battle Abbey, built on the spot where he fell during the Battle of Hastings in 1066.

rode bravely in front of his demoralized men, shouting, "Look at me! I am alive, and will be the victor with God's help!" His forces rallied and William was inspired to deploy the device of the feigned retreat—small detachments of Norman cavalry would pretend to flee, coaxing the Saxon infantry to break cover and rush forward in pursuit. The horsemen would then swing round and slaughter their pursuers. The tactic worked and severely weakened the English army. In the fading light of day, William's archers loosed a shower of arrows upon the defenders and King Harold fell to the ground, where he was slain by Norman swords. Harold's followers fled the scene and the battle was over. William erected his tent, enjoyed a victory feast, and settled down to spend the night surrounded by the bodies of those who had fallen. The next day was given over to the grisly task of burying the Norman dead, while the Saxon women began to remove the bodies of their slaughtered menfolk. Harold's mistress, Edith Swan-neck, identified his corpse by marks on his body known only to her. William refused Harold's mother her son's body for burial, and he was buried beneath a pile of rocks on the seashore, although his remains were later moved and given a Christian burial at Waltham Abbey.

In 1070, William ordered Battle Abbey to be built upon the site, and had the High Altar erected on the spot where Harold had fallen. That abbey is now a picturesque, evocative ruin, where Harold's bloodstained ghost is said to wander on the anniversary of the Battle of Hastings. There is an old belief that the ground hereabouts sweats blood whenever it rains, and that a fountain of blood sometimes spurts skyward from the site of the High Altar, in commemoration of the slaughter that took place here on that long-ago October day, when the course of English history was irrevocably changed.

ABOVE: The imposing gatehouse of Herstmonceux Castle, where a ghostly drummer has beaten his own death tattoo for centuries.

Hastings began. The English put up a fierce resistance, and Harold did "great execution" with his two-handed battle-axe. At one stage he even came close to winning when a rumor that William was dead swept through the Norman ranks causing them to break and retreat. But William removed his helmet, and

HERSTMONCEUX CASTLE
Herstmonceux, East Sussex

❈ ❈

This imposing castle was built in 1441 by Sir Roger de Fiennes and, although it is now occupied by a Canadian university, the grounds are open to the public and provide tantalizing glimpses of the red-brick, moated fortress that was restored to its original splendor in the early part of the 20th century. There is a tale, which dates back to its medieval occupancy, that one of Sir Roger's sons attempted to force himself upon a girl from the village, but met with valiant resistance. The girl escaped his clutches by leaping into the moat, but her ruthless attacker managed to catch hold of her

LEFT: A ghostly woman used to help American novelist Henry James with his writing whenever she visited him at his house in Rye.

and dragged her back into the castle, where he assaulted and then murdered her. This unfortunate girl is thought to be the spectral "white lady" whose silent wraith has been seen desperately swimming in the moat at night, or standing beside the water, wringing her shriveled hands in everlasting torment.

But the most famous shade to stir within the ancient walls is the "Phantom Drummer," who has been seen striding along the ramparts at night. Some say that he is the ghost of a 15th-century drummer, who died at the Battle of Agincourt and has beaten his own death tattoo ever since, with showers of blue sparks cascading from his glowing drumsticks. Other accounts name him as Lord Dacre, who feigned his death but continued to secretly live in the castle with his beautiful young wife. To deter the attentions of the numerous suitors who came to woo his supposed widow, he would apparently don a drummer's uniform; apply a liberal coating of phosphorous to his face, clothes, and drum; and appear as a fiendish phantom around the castle. Lord Dacre's wife is said to have eventually grown so tired of his deceit that she locked him in his room and starved him to death. Angered at the indignity of his demise, Lord Dacre's ghost has continued to patrol the castle and grounds ever since.

LAMB HOUSE
Rye, East Sussex
❈ ❈ ❈ ❈ ❈ ❈ ❈ ❈ ❈ ❈ ❈ ❈ ❈ ❈ ❈ ❈ ❈

This delightful, red-brick Queen Anne building was home to American-born writer Henry James from 1898 until his death in 1916. He claimed that he was frequently disturbed by poltergeist activity, and that he was often visited by the ghost of an old lady wearing a mantilla, who helped him with his writing. Although no one else ever saw this woman, an amateur photographer, who visited the building some time later, was surprised by the appearance of this spectral lady on one of the pictures he had taken. Following James's death, the author E. F. Benson became the tenant of the house, and he, too, was troubled by poltergeist activity. Sometime later, Rumer Godden, author of *Black Narcissus*, moved into the property. When the poltergeist activity started afresh, she called in a priest and had him "bless everything, including the fridge"!

ABOVE: The ghost ship *Lady Lovibond* sails onto the treacherous Goodwin Sands off the Kent Coast on February 13 every fifty years.

THE GOODWIN SANDS
Deal, Kent
❈ ❈

The Goodwin Sands are a series of banks that legend holds were once the fruitful lands of the ancient island of Lomera. They now lie several miles offshore and, although nearly always visible at low tide, are only safe to visit in June, when it is possible to take an organized excursion out to them. In

ABOVE: The haunted Dering Chapel in the church of St. Nicholas, Pluckley, where a dull knocking is often heard emanating from the burial vaults beneath the floor.

was well known in seafaring circles that it was unlucky to take a woman to sea. On this occasion, the danger was compounded by the fact that the ship's mate, a man named Rivers, had been a love rival for the woman, and the resentment of his rejection was seething within him as the fateful voyage began. As the ship sailed past the Goodwin Sands, his jealousy boiled over into a fit of uncontrollable rage. After murdering the helmsman, he steered the ship onto the sands, killing everyone on board.

Fifty years later, on February 13, 1798, the master of the coaster *Edenbridge* reported that he had almost collided with a three-masted schooner heading straight for the treacherous sands. On the same day in 1848, several witnesses reported sighting a schooner run aground on the notorious sands, but when the Deal lifeguards set out to rescue the crew, there was no trace of any ship. Traditionally the "ghost ship" of the Goodwin Sands appears every fifty years on the anniversary of the tragedy. Unfortunately, despite (or maybe even because of) the intense media and public interest that surrounded the forecast reenactment on February 13, 1998, the *Lady Lovibond* was conspicuous by its absence, and it will now be 2048 before the spectral schooner is due to make another dash for the ship-swallowing reaches of the Goodwin Sands.

PLUCKLEY
Pluckley, Kent
❆❆❆❆❆❆❆❆❆❆❆❆❆❆

Nestling amid the lush Kent countryside, Pluckley is a pretty and picturesque place that has long enjoyed the dubious reputation of being the most haunted village in England. Whereas this could, perhaps, be challenged by Prestbury in Gloucestershire (see page 41), there is no denying that many parts of this rural retreat are charged with a great deal of psychic energy, and many ghosts vie for attention in its churchyard, pubs, houses, and streets.

Many of the apparitions are related to the Dering family, lords of the manor from the 15th century until World War I. An intriguing remnant of their tenure can be seen

shipping circles, however, the very mention of their name has for centuries been sufficient to chill the blood of even the most hardened sailor. It is well known that these constantly shifting sands are always on the prowl, seeking to swallow ships and their crews. One of the worst disasters in British naval history occurred on and around these lurking banks on November 27, 1703. A whole fleet of English warships, commanded by Sir Cloudesley Shovel, were blown onto the sands during one of the worst storms that England has ever known. In total, thirteen ships and over 1,900 men and officers were lost that night, and the sea around the sands was littered with wreckage for weeks after.

But of all the numerous ships that have succumbed to the gluttonous appetite of these sinister sands, one in particular has ventured onto the hallowed plains of the haunted realm and sailed into popular mythology. The *Lady Lovibond* was a three-masted schooner. Its captain, Simon Peel, had recently married and had brought his wife, Annette, along on the voyage. Her presence had somewhat unnerved the crew, for it in the distinctive round-topped windows that grace so many of the buildings. During the Civil War, the staunchly Royalist Lord Dering escaped capture by Cromwell's forces by diving headlong through such a window. When he later came to rebuild his manor house, he commemorated the escape by having all the windows built in the same style, which was subsequently copied throughout the village.

The Derings have also left behind a more ethereal mark upon the village, particularly in the parish church of St. Nicholas. Many members of the family are buried in the Dering Chapel, inside which a strange dancing light has been seen and is often accompanied by a dull knocking that emanates from the burial vaults beneath the floor. In the early 1970s, a group of psychic researchers persuaded the then rector, the Reverend John Pittock, to allow them to spend a night locked inside the church. Armed with their cameras, tape recorders, and other necessary pieces of apparatus, they settled down to watch and wait. When the vicar came to let them out the next morning, they complained of having spent an uneventful night, the boredom of which had been alleviated only by the vicar's dog, who had come to visit them from time to time. "Actually," the vicar told them, "I don't have a dog!"

The churchyard is haunted by two females, who are thought to be the ghosts of members of the the Dering clan. There is the "Red Lady," whose baby is reputed to have died at birth and been buried in an unmarked grave, possibly because it was

BELOW: The ghosts of two women roam the churchyard of St. Nicholas's church in Pluckley, England's most haunted village.

illegitimate. She died shortly afterward, and ever since her wraith has wandered the churchyard, calling for her lost child. She shares her weary search with the "White Lady," whose beauty in life was such that, when she died at a tragically young age, her husband could not bear the thought of her body rotting away. He therefore had her dressed in a priceless gown and placed inside an airtight lead coffin, a single red rose upon her breast. Her coffin was then sealed inside a number of other airtight coffins, which were encased in a casket of solid oak and buried inside a deep vault. But despite her tomb, on misty autumn mornings she breaks free from her confines and manifests in the churchyard, her flowing black hair providing a striking contrast to the brilliant white of her gown, as she clutches in her hand a single red rose.

Near to the church is the Black Horse Inn, built in the 14th century and haunted by a ghostly prankster, who delights in hiding the personal possessions of staff and customers alike. Glasses have been known to move slowly across shelves of their own accord, and an unseen hand has sometimes lifted cutlery and arranged it neatly on the bar. A short distance from the inn and church is Station Road, where a feeling of

ABOVE: The twin towers of St. Mary's church, Reculver, from where a ghostly wailing infant is heard on storm-tossed nights.

OPPOSITE: The Shipwrights Arms, near Faversham has a phantom sailor as its oldest "regular."

melancholic desperation is said to pervade the air. It is particularly noticeable between a large white house known as Greystones, and a pretty house called Rose Court that stands nearby. According to tradition, a 16th-century monk who lived on the site now occupied by Greystones fell in love with a woman living at Rose Court, who was also the mistress of a member of the Dering family. Whenever they could, the two would meet and walk together in the nearby lanes, accompanied by the woman's small dog. However, the lady found the love triangle so distressing that she killed herself with a fatal cocktail distilled from poisoned berries. The grief-stricken monk then pined away, dying soon after of a broken heart. Many people walking along Station Road have heard the playful yapping of an invisible dog, which has been followed by the cheerful chatting of a man and woman. Closer and closer the spectral voices get until, when they are virtually upon the startled witnesses, they pass briskly by and then fade away further along the road.

On the outskirts of the village is the aptly named "Fright Corner," where a highwayman once made his last desperate stand with his back to an oak tree that stood here until quite recently. Finally overcome by his adversaries, he was pinned to the tree by the cold steel of several swords. Startled witnesses have frequently seen a replay of his last battle in the fading light of winters' days, and some drivers have been astonished when their headlights suddenly illuminate his bloody specter pinned against a large phantom tree.

A little way across the fields from the village is the Elvey Farm Country Hotel. Originally built as a barn in the 1400s, an upper story was added in the 16th century, and it was later converted into a comfortable home. In the days when the building was a farmhouse, there were frequent sightings of a young fair-haired man with a short-cropped beard. Doors opened mysteriously in the night, phantom footsteps were heard plodding along corridors, and lights were switched on by unseen hands. There is a tradition that a tenant farmer committed suicide at the farm in the 1850s, following the death of his wife and the failure of his business. Intriguingly, a Japanese television crew who visited the hotel in the 1990s brought with them a medium to contact whatever spirits haunted the building. No sooner had the medium climbed out of the car than she felt the overwhelming sensation of someone drowning—she could not have known that the car park stands on the site of a pond that was filled in long ago.

RECULVER TOWERS
Reculver, Kent

The dramatic twin towers of St. Mary's church are built upon the site of the Roman fort Regulbium, dating from the 3rd century. For many years there have been reports of the ghostly sounds of a wailing infant coming from the ruins on stormy, windswept nights. Folklore had always maintained that the spectral howling was the result of the Romans having buried a baby alive as a sacrifice when the fort was built.

Archeology appeared to lend credence to the legend when, in the 1960s, an excavation of the site uncovered the skeletons of no fewer than eleven babies, interred either in or beneath the walls of the Roman fort. In the latter years of the 20th century, there were constant reports of two hooded figures moving around and between the two towers at night. When approached, both figures would melt away into nothingness.

THE SHIPWRIGHTS ARMS
Faversham, Kent

An isolated and remote setting amid marshland and mud flats lends this three-hundred-year-old, weatherboarded hostelry an eerie and timeless aura. It is a single-bar pub adorned with nautical fittings, in which the wraith of an old sea dog has been making a decided nuisance of himself for as long as anyone can remember. When the chill winds of winter hurl themselves relentlessly at the walls and windows, the thick-set phantom sailor, who has glowing red eyes and wears a heavy reefer jacket with a peaked cap, has frequently appeared to chill the blood of numerous landlords, landladies, and customers. His ghostly jaunts are always presaged by the overwhelming smell of rum, tar, and tobacco, and his passage is marked by a distinct nip in the air. Tradition tells us that in life he was the captain of a 19th-century ship that foundered and sank in the Swale. Managing to clamber onto the mud flats, he dragged himself toward the lights of a little weatherboarded cottage that he could see in the distance. Cold and exhausted, he banged upon the door. Unwilling to answer his door at such a late hour, the owner shouted at him to go away. On rising the next morning, he found the stranger dead on the doorstep. It would appear that he also, unwittingly, admitted the captain's spirit, which has been resident ever since.

A former landlady awoke many times to find the phantom sailor standing at the bottom of her bed, glaring at her. He has also been seen in a small room that adjoins the bar. Many customers have been startled when the bearded phantom suddenly enters and then vanishes right in front of them. But the most bizarre experience must be that of a former landlord's son, Barry Tester, who, on a cold winter's night, awoke to find that the ghostly "Jack Tar" had climbed into bed with him!

The
WITCH
COUNTIES

They say that the Dead die not, but remain
Near to the rich heirs of their grief and mirth.
I think they ride the calm midheaven, as these,
In wise majestic melancholy train,
And watch the moon, and the still raging seas,
And men, coming and going on the earth.

FROM *CLOUDS*

BY RUPERT BROOKE

Essex, Suffolk, Norfolk, & Cambridgeshire

It is a sad fact that during the witchcraft hysteria of the 16th and 17th centuries, more people were executed in the counties that comprise the old kingdom of East Anglia than in any other part of the country. This was partly as a result of the Puritan stranglehold on the district, whereby holy water had been outlawed and exorcism abolished, leaving the God-fearing people of the area to think that they were defenseless against the devil and other evil spirits in which they still believed. The area is rich in legend, and its superstitions were rooted in Danish lore. All in all, the contrasts and history of the "witch counties" offer a surprising amount of variety and a genuine sense of isolation that make them fascinating.

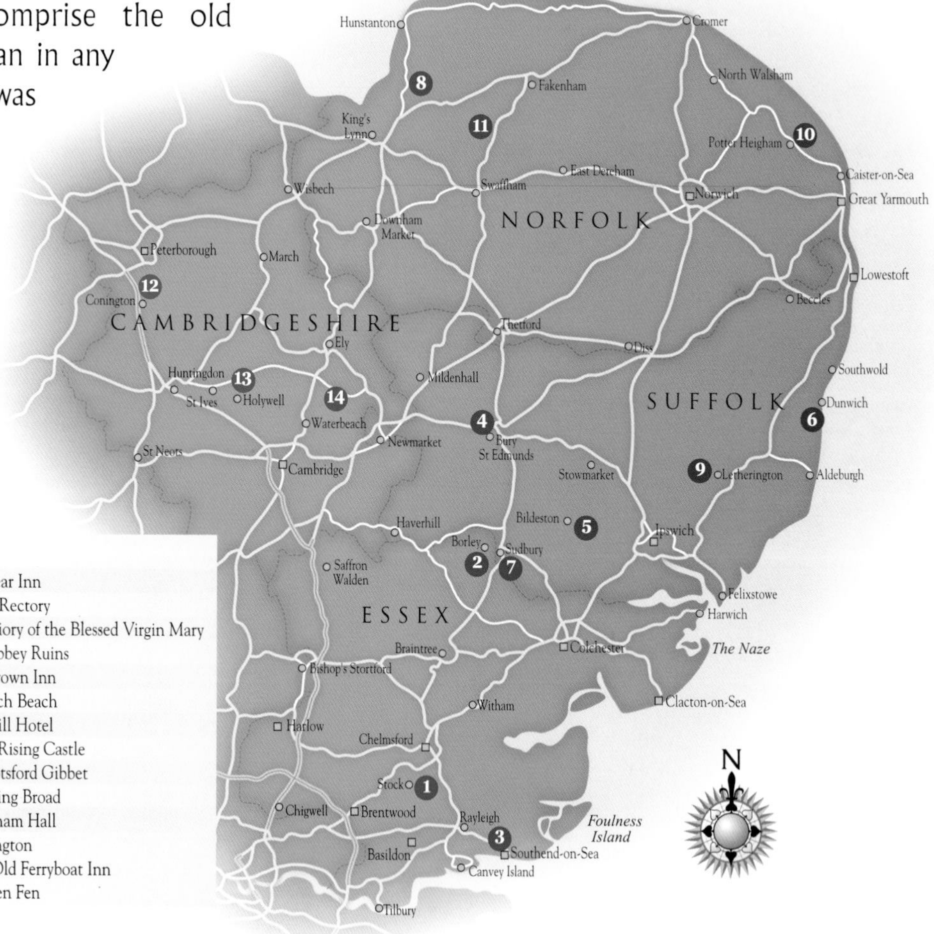

KEY
1. The Bear Inn
2. Borley Rectory
3. The Priory of the Blessed Virgin Mary
4. The Abbey Ruins
5. The Crown Inn
6. Dunwich Beach
7. The Mill Hotel
8. Castle Rising Castle
9. The Potsford Gibbet
10. Hickling Broad
11. Raynham Hall
12. Conington
13. The Old Ferryboat Inn
14. Wicken Fen

The Bear Inn
Stock, Essex

The Bear Inn, located in the charming Essex village of Stock, is one of those pubs where time passes ever so slowly. It is a white-painted, gabled old building, with tall Tudor chimneys and a sloping, red-tiled roof. At any time of the day or night, you are sure to find a knowledgeable local supping a pint at the bar, who is more than happy to while away a summer's afternoon or winter's evening, telling you in hushed tones "all about the ghost."

Charlie Marshall was the ostler at this four-hundred-year-old inn during the closing years of the 19th century. He was a small, wiry man, whose strange sideways walk earned him the nickname "Spider." When drunk, he had the peculiar habit of

PREVIOUS PAGES: Raynham Hall, the historic haunt of an infamous "brown lady."

crawling up the taproom chimney and emerging, covered in soot, from the fireplace of the next bar. This extraordinary feat led to him becoming something of a local celebrity, and people would often visit the inn just to watch him perform. One Christmas Eve, having set off up the chimney, he took it into his head not to come down, but just sat in a bacon-curing loft at the junction of the two chimneys, ignoring the increasingly hostile entreaties of his employer and workmates to "come on down." Exasperated, his colleagues decided to encourage his descent by lighting a small fire in the grate, the smoke from which suffocated old Spider. His well-cured remains are supposedly still up in the junction of the two chimneys today! Spider's ghost, though, often descends at night. Dressed in white breeches and shiny leather boots, he flits about the nooks and shadowy recesses of the old inn, still possessing that strange, sideways gait that earned him his nickname.

BELOW: The long-vanished rectory at Borley, whose posthumous fame still brings ghost hunters flocking to the tiny village on the Suffolk/Essex border.

Borley Rectory

Borley, Essex

Nothing now survives of the building that was once dubbed "the most haunted house in England," save occasional piles of crumbling brick that lie buried beneath nettles and weeds. Local residents have long since grown weary of the dubious honor that their long-gone rectory has foisted upon them, and today, one of the most bizarre things about the village is how difficult it is to find. Few signposts exist to point the intrepid ghost hunter in the right direction. The village church is kept locked to deter the overenthusiasm of the numerous visitors to whom the village has long been a place of pilgrimage. Should you dare ask any of the villagers about the current status of the haunting, you are liable to receive a decidedly frosty reaction.

In paranormal circles the events at the old rectory are still the subject of intense debate, while those who continue to

ABOVE: Harry Price (1881–1948) whose investigations at the old rectory led to it being dubbed the "most haunted house in England."

find their way to this little corner of rural England, on the Essex and Suffolk border, often report strange sightings and inexplicable happenings.

The not particularly attractive red-brick rectory was built in 1863 by the Reverend Henry Bull on, tradition maintains, part of the site of a medieval monastery. Legend tells of an illicit love affair between one of the monks and a nun from the nearby convent at Bures. Their planned elopement was discovered, and both were condemned to death for their misdemeanor. The monk was hanged, but the nun was bricked up alive in the cellars of the monastery. Thereafter, her ghostly form was often reported drifting over the place where her earthly remains were reputedly entombed.

At first, she seems to have been a conventional ghostly nun, one of hundreds condemned to roam the ethereal plains of Britain for committing similar transgressions with lusty clerics. But the building of the rectory in 1863 across the route of her ghostly jaunts seems to have stirred her to indignation, and she made her displeasure known from the outset. Many was the occasion when family members would look up from the dinner table to see her mournful face watching them through the window. Indignant at the ghostly stalker's rudeness, the Reverend Bull had the window bricked up! Unperturbed, the phantom sister unleashed a bout of poltergeist activity around the house. The ghostly happenings grew more and more dramatic, and by the time Henry Bull was succeeded as rector by his son, Harry, in 1892, they were interfering with the everyday running of the house. Several servants refused to work in a place where a ghostly coach could, at any moment, come tearing across the dining room, pass through the wall, and disappear on the lawn outside! Such was the house's terrible reputation that when Harry died in 1927, no fewer than twelve clergymen turned down the post of rector.

In 1928, the Reverend G. E. Smith and his wife, both avowed skeptics, moved into the empty building. Within weeks, the haunting had flared up again. The phantom nun continued with her nocturnal wanderings, but she had apparently now been joined by the ghost of Harry Bull himself. Mysterious footsteps would echo from empty rooms in the dead of night. Strange, incoherent whispering would be heard, and the voice of an invisible woman would moan softly, its low murmur growing louder and louder until, following a sudden scream of "Don't Carlos, don't," the house would again become quiet.

In June 1929, the *Daily Mirror* published the story of the sinister happenings at Borley. Harry Price, founder and honorary director of the National Laboratory of Psychical Research, read the article with excited fascination. On June 12, 1929, he visited the rectory and began an investigation that would catapult the remote Essex village into the international spotlight.

The spirits responded to his arrival with a veritable array of ghostly phenomena. Phantom fingers tapped out messages on a mirror; invisible hands smashed vases against walls; keys leapt from keyholes and were thrown to the floor; a tempest of household objects came raining down the staircase; a window pane was broken; and one disgruntled wraith even hurled a candlestick at Harry Price's head.

In July 1929, the Smiths had had enough and moved out, and it wasn't until October 1930 that a new rector could be found. His name was Lionel Algernon Foyster, a relative of the original owner, and the dark forces at work within the house marked his arrival with an intensification of activity. An invisible assailant struck his wife, Marianne, hard across the face; objects disappeared and were either never seen again or would reappear in the most bizarre locations.

Harry Price was asked to resume his investigations, and on his first night, as he sat down to dinner with the family, the ghosts welcomed him by turning the wine to ink. But the phenomenon that most intrigued Price was the appearance of the so-called "Marianne Messages." Addressed to the rector's young wife, these strange, often-illegible scribbles appeared upon the walls, imploring her to "please get help."

By 1937, the Reverend Foyster and his family had moved out, and Harry Price decided he would lease the building for a year. His newspaper advertisement for assistants drew two hundred replies, of whom forty were chosen to help with the subsequent investigation. In the course of a séance, a spirit claiming to be Harry Bull said that the bodies of a nun and a monk, named Fadenoch, were buried in the garden. Another spirit, claiming to be the dead nun, identified herself as Marie Lairre and told how she had been enticed to Borley from France by a man from the local and influential Waldengrave

RIGHT: Ghostly messages were just one of the phenomena to haunt Borley Rectory.

BELOW: The church and churchyard at Borley, where strange occurrences are still reported.

ABOVE: The moldering abbey ruins at Bury St. Edmunds, where monastic feet once shuffled in peaceful contemplation and shadowy figures now walk by the light of a full moon.

family. She went on to inform the gathering how she had wished to marry him, but that he had strangled her and buried her body beneath the cellar. At a further séance, a spirit calling itself Sunex Amures informed the sitters that the rectory would be burned down that very night. Nothing, however, happened.

When Price left the house in 1938 a new tenant, Captain W. H. Gregson, moved in and renamed it The Priory. On February 27, 1939, he was sorting books in the hall when a stack toppled over and upset a paraffin lamp. In the ensuing conflagration, several onlookers claimed to have seen writhing figures moving around in the flames, and the ghostly form of a nun standing in one of the burning windows. In 1943, Harry Price returned to the ruins where, three feet beneath the cellar floor, his excavations uncovered the bones of a young woman. Price died in 1948 and, ever since, debate has raged in paranormal circles as to whether the saga was a genuine haunting, or nothing more than a cleverly orchestrated fraud.

Reports of ghostly sightings in the little churchyard, however, still continue. The phantom nun maintains her weary regime of nocturnal strolls along "Nun's Walk." The village church and its surrounds are as eerie as ever, and many visitors speak of a sudden feeling of foreboding that grips them the moment they set foot in the neat, though neglected, little churchyard.

Ghostly organ music has often been heard wailing from inside the empty church. Investigators have recorded phantom footsteps, mysterious tappings, and even a harsh, menacing cry that sends shivers down the spines of those who listen to the

tape. Many photographs taken of the building's exterior have, when developed, contained ghostly forms standing among the sunken graves or gliding along the uneven paths of what is still one of England's spookiest places.

THE PRIORY OF THE BLESSED VIRGIN MARY
Prittlewell, Essex

The remains of the priory are now incorporated into a delightful museum, where a ghostly monk is said to roam on certain nights. In the restored Prior's Chamber, a curious stone is displayed, on which the twisted features of an agonized face are clearly discernible. The face is supposedly that of a medieval priest named Rainaldus, who, having sold his soul to the devil, found himself possessed by that worthy. One day, as he celebrated mass at St. Mary's church in the nearby village of Runwell, the devil suddenly emerged from his mouth, causing such a fearful tempest that the parishioners fled in terror. When they returned with another priest, all that remained of Rainaldus was a bubbling pool of dark liquid, at the center of which lay this stone face, its hollow eyes, squashed nose, and tormented features frozen in eternal horror.

THE ABBEY RUINS
Bury St. Edmunds, Suffolk

The site of the old Benedictine abbey was once the resting place of the remains of St. Edmund, Suffolk's martyr-king who was killed by Danish invaders in 870 when he refused to recant his Christian faith. By the time of the Reformation, his shrine had achieved such prominence as a place of pilgrimage that it was second only to that of Thomas à Becket at Canterbury. But during the dissolution of the monasteries, the tomb was desecrated, and the abbey was dissolved in 1539.

Today, the passage of time has left the once proud arches of what must have been a spectacular building moldering in decay. Its haunting buttresses have tottered and fallen. Its stark stone columns now loom over eerie, crumbling walls, while hollow windows look mournfully down on the shattered cloisters and scattered aisles, where monastic feet once shuffled in peaceful contemplation. But when the glint of a full moon casts dancing shadows across the ruins, ghostly monks have been known to walk amid the once proud walls, or to stand silently by the old gatehouse of what is acknowledged to be one the most spiritually charged locations in England.

THE CROWN INN
Bildstone, Suffolk

❈❈❈❈❈❈❈❈❈❈❈❈❈❈❈❈❈❈❈❈

The timeless aura that descends upon you as you enter this 15th-century inn, with its inglenook fireplace and low beams, is quaintly reminiscent of a bygone and long-lost age. Sitting in its snug and atmospheric bar, listening to the low murmur of the conversation, it is easy to close your eyes and cast your imagination back over the literally thousands of events to which its ancient walls must have borne witness. There was the infamous election campaign of 1855, when The Crown was being used as a political headquarters by one of the candidates, and rival supporters attacked the inn. They shattered the windows, smashed crockery, broke many of the drinking vessels, and then, with their frustrations vented, proceeded with a noble attempt to drink the pub dry! If your mind ventures back further into the foggy mists of time, you can imagine the excitement of the wool merchant's family, for whom the property was first built, when they moved into

their brand-new home in the year 1495. Then, if you open your eyes, you may just catch a glimpse of one of the many ghosts that flit about its rooms.

A mysterious "gray lady" has been seen at a window that looks out onto the car park, waving a ghostly farewell to departing customers. Two children, dressed in Victorian outfits, have appeared before startled guests at various points around the inn, while an old man in a tricornered hat is frequently seen sitting in a favored corner of the main bar. For those who enjoy a smattering of haunted hospitality, Room Four is the bedroom in which guests often experience things going bump in the dead of night. They may be treated to an appearance of the gray lady, or of the "genial missionary," whose presence has been detected by several visiting mediums. If neither of these is sufficient to aid a decent night's unrest, there are always the ice-cold fingers that have been known to stroke the necks of sleeping guests.

DUNWICH BEACH
Suffolk

❈❈❈❈❈❈❈❈❈❈❈❈❈❈❈❈❈❈❈❈

What was once the sixth-largest town in England is now little more than a tiny, albeit atmospheric, coastal village, where to

BELOW: Much of the town of Dunwich now lies beneath the relentless waters of the North Sea. But the ghosts of long-dead citizens are said to walk along its shingle beach and crumbling cliffs at twilight.

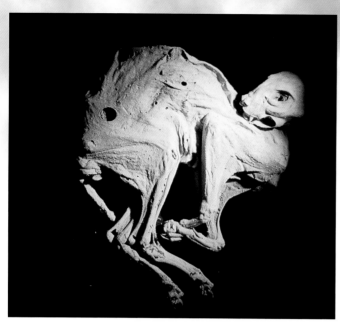

ABOVE: The grisly remains of a mummified cat greet visitors to The Mill Hotel in Sudbury. Attempts to remove it have frequently led to spates of bad luck.

stride along the shoreline at twilight is to feel the true thrill of haunted England. The gulls wheel about you, their raucous cries intermingling with the thunderous percussion of the crashing waves. Legend speaks of these birds being the souls of long-dead fishermen.

History tells that the once great town of Dunwich now lies submerged beneath the foaming waters of the very sea that stretches out before you. In a quiet moment, when the gulls fall silent and the wild waves retreat to prepare their next assault, you may just hear the ghostly bells of the town's churches, tolling their mournful knell from beneath the swell, their dull chimes drifting upon the sea breeze. You may even spy the nebulous wraiths of long-dead citizens, whose restless spirits are said to walk the clifftops when darkness falls. And you will feel in that moment of peaceful solitude that you have truly walked with ghosts on Dunwich shore.

THE MILL HOTEL
Sudbury, Suffolk
❆❆❆❆❆❆❆❆❆❆❆❆❆❆❆❆❆❆❆❆❆❆❆❆

This picturesque hotel, with its white, weatherboarded facade, stands over a tranquil reach of the River Stour. The wheel from the days when the building was a mill has survived the ravages of time and can still be seen encased in glass. But entombed beneath the floor of the hotel reception, is a gruesome artifact, upon which the very fortunes of the ancient property may well depend.

It is a mummified cat that had apparently been walled up alive in the roof of the original building. The unfortunate

creature was discovered in 1971 during building work to convert the property into a hotel. It was once common to entomb cats within the walls or foundations of newly erected buildings, since it was widely believed that their presence would then protect the structure from both fire and ill luck.

Following its discovery, the cat was removed from the building and taken to a nearby studio. Soon afterward, a heavy wooden beam suddenly collapsed, causing a great deal of structural damage to the hotel. No sooner had the necessary repairs been carried out than financial problems halted the building work for a time. When the studio to which the cat had been removed mysteriously caught fire, it was decided by the owners that there might be something in the old superstition, and the cat was returned to the hotel, where it can still be seen today, through a glass panel in the floor.

A further spate of bad luck befell the property when the feline charm was again removed in 1999 to allow necessary repair work to be carried out. Over the two-week period, the road outside exploded, the manager's office flooded several times, and the person who had removed the creature met with an accident. Once the cat was returned to its resting place, all was well again.

CASTLE RISING CASTLE
Castle Rising, Norfolk
❆❆❆❆❆❆❆❆❆❆❆❆❆❆❆❆❆❆❆❆❆❆❆❆

Defensively situated atop its prodigious man-made earthworks of massive ramparts and deep ditches, Castle Rising Castle boasts an impressive pedigree that stretches back to 1140, when the magnificent Norman keep was built by William Albini to celebrate his marriage to the widow of Henry I. Over the next four hundred years, it evolved into a magnificent residence until, following the execution of its then owner, the Duke of Norfolk, in 1572, it was abandoned and became little more than a ruin, its walls made precarious by a proliferation of rabbits burrowing into its great earthen banks.

Today, the castle ruin is as impressive as ever, and can be numbered among the largest and most ornate in England. Ascending the great stone staircase and passing into the keep, one is greeted by twisting corridors and passageways which lead to a fascinating sequence of rooms, galleries, and tiny staircases. The upper rooms are said to be haunted by the ghost of one of the castle's most notorious former residents, Isabella, "the she-wolf of France."

As the former mistress of Roger Mortimer, Queen Isabella was instrumental in the deposition and horrific murder of her husband, Edward II, in 1327 (see page 40). It is a widely held misconception that Isabella's son, Edward III, following

RIGHT: The maniacal ghostly cacklings of Queen Isabella are said to echo through the ruins of Castle Rising Castle.

the execution of her accomplice, Roger Mortimer, imprisoned her at the castle in 1331. Rather, Isabella lived in regal splendor at Castle Rising and was free to move with her retinue between her various residences, as befitted a lady of social standing. Legend states that this formidable woman sank into an old age that was racked by violent dementia, her last troubled years being spent in the whitewashed rooms of the upper stories. She died at her castle in Hertford on August 23, 1358, and was buried in the monastery of the Greyfriars, by Newgate in London.

The echoes of Isabella's last troubled years, however, are still said to rebound through the eerie corridors of Castle Rising Castle. Several visitors have been shocked to hear the sound of hysterical cackling around the top floor of the building, while residents in the nearby village have occasionally been disturbed by ghostly screams and maniacal laughter coming from the castle in the early hours of the morning.

THE POTSFORD GIBBET
Letheringham, Suffolk
❀ ❀ ❀ ❀ ❀ ❀ ❀ ❀ ❀ ❀ ❀ ❀ ❀ ❀ ❀ ❀ ❀ ❀

Potsford Wood is an eerie place, even on the brightest of summer days. But on a wild, winter's night, it is truly frightening. The skeletal trees stand gaunt and shadowy, their creaking branches interlocking with one another in grim embrace. Their menacing canopy, which shields the wood from the moon's dull glow, causes an aura of foreboding to hang heavy in the air, and the wood enjoys a sinister and eerie reputation. One spot in particular inspires terror in those who venture into it.

Almost lost amid its creeping carpets of nettle and bracken are the decaying remains of the Potsford Gibbet, last used on April 14, 1699, when Jonah Snell was executed here for the murder of a local miller, John Bullard, and his son. It is around this rotting remnant that people, walking along the road outside the wood at night, have noticed strange, twinkling lights hovering in midair. They have been startled to see a sinister, dark shape standing by the gibbet, its appearance often accompanied by a choking groan.

Even the warmth of a summer's day is no protection against the malevolent forces loose in Potsford Wood. Several people, while enjoying a pleasant country stroll when the sun blazes overhead, have paused to gaze upon the curious remains of the old gibbet. Turning to resume their ramble, they have been surprised to find a dark figure standing behind them. To their horror, they notice that beneath the hooded cloak, there is a grimacing, hollow-eyed skull staring back at them!

HICKLING BROAD
Potter Higham, Norfolk
❀ ❀

In summer, the picturesque waters of Hickling Broad are a congested tangle of every conceivable type of sailing vessel. But when the chill of winter has turned the rippling waters to ice, and a keen wind howls through the dark days and nights, the rhythmic tattoo of a distant drum is sometimes heard beating from the depths of the frozen Broad, as the phantom drummer sets out on his eternal search for his long-lost love.

In the winter prior to the Battle of Waterloo, a poor drummer boy met and fell in love with the daughter of a rich and influential man of the neighborhood. She reciprocated his advances, but her father frowned upon the relationship and forbade her to see the young man. Ignoring her father's wishes, the girl would sneak out each evening and make her way to a small hut on the edge of Hickling Broad, where her soldier-love would skate across the frozen waters to join her, sounding his approach by playing a rhythmic tattoo upon his kettle drum. But one cold February night, as the girl listened to the sound of the drum that marked his approach, the beat suddenly ceased. The ice had given way and sent the boy plunging to his death in the cold depths of the freezing waters.

And so it is that, as darkness rolls across Hickling Broad on cold and misty February evenings, the phantom drummer still beats his mournful tattoo, as his shivering specter skates from the gloom to search for the girl whose heart was his, but whose spirit he lost long, long ago.

RAYNHAM HALL
Fakenham, Norfolk
❀ ❀

Raynham Hall, the seat of the Marquesses of Townshend, has been the haunt of the mysterious "Brown Lady" for more than two hundred and fifty years. It is generally accepted, though by no means proven, that she is the ghost of Dorothy Walpole, wife of the second Marquess, and daughter of England's first Prime Minister, Sir Robert Walpole.

Dorothy was twenty-six years old when she married Lord Charles Townshend in 1712. They had been childhood sweethearts but, since her father had also been the boy's legal guardian, he had originally refused to allow them to marry, lest it be generally presumed that he was trying to benefit from such a union. So, Townshend went on to marry someone else, and Dorothy became the mistress of the thoroughly dissolute Lord Wharton, who was later forced to flee the country to avoid his creditors. When Townshend's wife died in 1711, he and Dorothy rekindled their relationship, and were married in 1712. Unfortunately, Dorothy had kept the details of her affair secret from her new husband, who found out about it quite by accident and, in his fury, locked his wife in her chambers at Raynham Hall. She died in 1726, officially of smallpox, unofficially of a broken heart or—according to legend—of a broken neck following a mysterious fall down the grand staircase.

Ever since, Dorothy's ghost has made frequent visits. In the early 19th century, King George IV stayed at the hall and was given the state bedroom. Waking in the early hours of the morning, he saw a woman in a brown dress standing by his bed. It so terrified him that he would not spend "another hour in this accursed house."

The Victorian author, Captain Marryat, was walking along a corridor of the hall one night, accompanied by two of Lord Townshend's nephews. Suddenly, they observed a woman coming toward them, and since they were wearing their nightclothes, they modestly hid behind a door. The woman carried a lamp, the light from which illuminated her dress, showing that it was made from brown fabric. Passing by, she turned her head and glanced at them in what Marryat called a "diabolical manner." The captain was carrying a pistol, which he fired at the dreadful apparition. To his horror, the bullet simply passed through her, and the woman disappeared. The bullet was later found embedded in a door behind the spot where the ghost had been standing.

In September 1936, Lady Townshend commissioned Indre Shira to take photographs of the hall's interior. He and his assistant, Mr. Provand, were about to shoot the grand staircase when "a vapory form, which gradually assumed the appearance of a woman draped in a veil," appeared on the

ABOVE: The ghostly photograph taken on the staircase at Raynham Hall in 1936.

bottom flight. Shira shouted to Provand to take a picture. Although Provand could not see anything, he aimed his camera at the staircase and snapped. When the negative was developed, a ghostly outline of a human figure appeared.

The photograph caused a sensation when it was published in *Country Life* magazine on December 1, 1936. Experts have subjected it to intense scrutiny, but no evidence of fakery has ever been discovered. Ghost investigator Robert Thurston Hopkins described it as "the most genuine ghost photograph we possess, and no study of the supernatural is complete without reference to it."

"THE MOST GENUINE GHOST PHOTOGRAPH WE POSSESS"

ROBERT THURSTON HOPKINS ON SHIRA'S PHOTOGRAPH AT RAYNHAM HALL

CONINGTON
nr Peterborough, Cambridgeshire

❀❀❀❀❀❀❀❀❀❀❀❀❀❀❀❀❀❀❀❀❀❀

As the London-bound express trains thunder at ever-increasing speeds past the Cambridgeshire village of Conington, they race over a tiny crossing that a series of tragic accidents has endowed with such a sinister reputation that it has been branded "the crossing of death." In the 1940s, six German prisoners of war were killed here when a light engine plowed into the truck in which they were traveling early one foggy Monday morning. On the afternoon of October 16, 1948, Colonel A. H. Mellows was driving his black Chrysler car toward the crossing at around 5:30 p.m. After stopping to allow his passenger, Mr. A. F. Percival, to get out of the car to open the gates, the colonel edged his vehicle forward, straight into the path of a London-bound express. The train plowed into the colonel's car, killing both him and his dog. Colonel Mellows was buried with full civic honors, and his dog was laid to rest alongside the stretch of track where the tragic accident had taken place.

Needless to say, with such a dreadful history the crossing soon acquired a reputation for being haunted. Signalmen who were assigned the box at Conington would often hear the sound of locked gates apparently being opened and closed; sometimes they would catch ephemeral glimpses of a large black car approaching the crossing, but it would have disappeared by the time they arrived to open the gates. The aptly named Mr. Norman Jinks, who was in charge of the signal box throughout the 1960s, frequently heard the distinctive sound of ghostly tires crunching across the gravel, although no car was ever visible. The signal box was removed in the 1970s, ostensibly for technical rather than supernatural reasons, but people still avoid the "crossing of death" when the lengthening shadows of night stretch across the remote and windswept expanse of Conington Fen.

ABOVE: The reputed tomb of 11th-century suicide Juliet Tewslie in the Old Ferry Boat Inn. Her ghostly figure is reputed to rise from it at midnight on March 17 each year.

THE OLD FERRY BOAT INN
Holywell, Cambridgeshire

❀❀❀❀❀❀❀❀❀❀❀❀❀❀❀❀❀❀❀❀❀❀

An isolated setting on the leafy banks of the Great Ouse and a thatched roof over ancient oak beams, beneath which massive inglenook fireplaces blaze a warm welcome, all help make the Old Ferry Boat Inn one of Cambridgeshire's most atmospheric hostelries. Its stone floor now lies hidden beneath a plush carpet—except, that is, one rectangular slab of ancient granite which the owners would never dare cover, for beneath it are said to rest the mortal remains of Juliet Tewslie.

Neglected by her lover Tom, the inconsolable Juliet is said to have hanged herself on March 17 in, approximately, 1078. On finding Juliet's body, Tom was overcome with grief and remorse. He cut her down, cradled her lifeless form in his arms and, having bade her a sorrowful farewell, buried her where she died, marking the grave with the block of granite over which the Old Ferry Boat Inn was later built.

The evening of March 17 each year is something of a party night at the inn. The first chimes of midnight are said to bring Juliet Tewslie rising from her grave to float around the pub. And such is her posthumous fame that her

appearance is eagerly awaited by locals, international ghost hunters, or the just plain curious, who come flocking in their thousands to greet the poor girl whose tragic demise, and subsequent nocturnal jaunts, have made her one of Cambridgeshire's most abiding annual fixtures.

WICKEN FEN
Cambridgeshire
❀ ❀ ❀ ❀ ❀ ❀ ❀ ❀ ❀ ❀ ❀ ❀ ❀

Wicken Fen, near the village of Wicken, has changed little since the days when Hereward the Wake roamed its marshy expanse battling against the Norman invaders. It is a strangely primeval place, and a definite sense of chilling unease ripples through its seven-hundred mysterious acres. At night, its wild avenues of beech and rowan tower over beds of giant reeds, through which the breeze whispers eerily, and where the sudden movement of a tiny mammal is easily mistaken for the advance of something that could have far more sinister, inexplicable overtones.

Could these overtones be the strange, twisting shades of Roman legionaries, perhaps? For the legionaries have been known to suddenly materialize before startled witnesses and then melt back, just as suddenly, into the silent shadows. Battles fought long ago are still repeated by phantom armies that are heard though never seen. A sinister black dog wades through the dark waters, its eyes fixed on an unseen prey. But of all the sinister specters that roam this forlorn wilderness,

ABOVE: A sense of chilling unease ripples through the seven hundred mysterious acres of Wicken Fen, and many ghosts roam its marshy expanse.

few are more feared than those known as the "lantern men." These strange, inexplicable lights that dance and twist over the dark surface of the great mere, or skip erratically in and out of the reed beds, are said to be evil spirits whose sole intent is to lure unsuspecting mortals to a hideous death deep within their marshy domain.

DEMONIC LORDS
and SATAN'S SORCERY

Thou art the whisper in the gloom,
The hinting tone, the haunting laugh:
Thou art the adorner of my tomb,
The minstrel of mine epitaph.

FROM *THE DARK ANGEL*
BY LIONEL JOHNSON

Northamptonshire, Leicester-shire, Lincolnshire, Notting-hamshire, & West midlands

The counties that stretch from the Lincolnshire coast to the flat and arable pastures of the East and West Midlands are steeped in some of the best-known legends of English history. Who can wander the byways of Nottinghamshire without giving a thought to the world's most famous outlaw, Robin Hood? And who can gaze upon the great expanse of Bosworth Field without conjuring up vivid images of the hunchbacked figure of Shakespeare's Richard III, scheming his way though a winter of discontent, only to end up desperate to exchange his king-dom for a life-saving mount?

Witchcraft and its perceived effects are much in evidence across the landscape, and a tomb in the pretty parish church at Bottesford, Leicestershire, even tells of two boys being killed by "wicked practice and sorcerye." Further south, the county of Northamptonshire is indelibly linked with the fate of Mary, Queen of Scots, whose beheading at the long-demolished Fotheringay Castle launched what is, arguably, the busiest ghost upon Britain's spectral landscape.

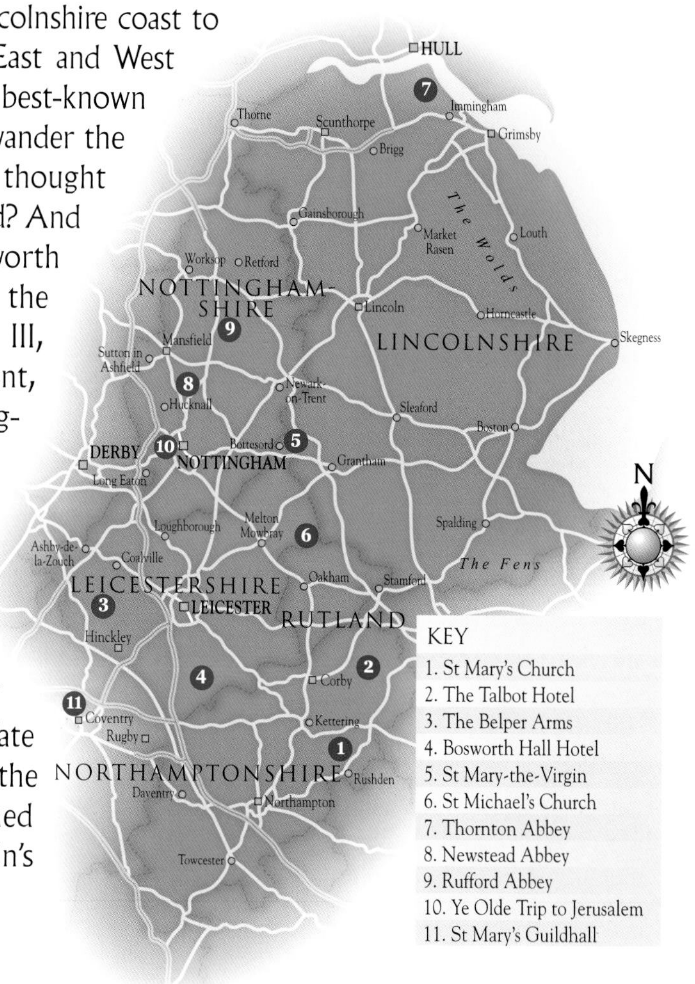

KEY

1. St Mary's Church
2. The Talbot Hotel
3. The Belper Arms
4. Bosworth Hall Hotel
5. St Mary-the-Virgin
6. St Michael's Church
7. Thornton Abbey
8. Newstead Abbey
9. Rufford Abbey
10. Ye Olde Trip to Jerusalem
11. St Mary's Guildhall

ST. MARY'S CHURCH
Woodford, Northamptonshire

A curious relic can be found in the picturesque church of St. Mary's in Woodford. In the late 1540s, the then vicar of the church, John Styles, lost his parish due to his Catholic sympathies. Taking with him an expensive and ornate chalice, he fled to a monastery in Belgium, but died shortly after his arrival. A later incumbent at the church, Andrew Powlet,

PREVIOUS PAGES: Who can travel the road to Bosworth Field without thinking of Richard III's desperate plight?

succeeded in retrieving the costly ornament and brought it back to the parish with, for some reason, the heart of John Styles. In time, both relics disappeared and were little more than an archaic memory when, in 1862, Powlet's ghost was spotted standing by a particular panel in the wall of the rectory. An examination of the spot revealed a secret chamber which contained the chalice and a letter, which led to the discovery of the well-traveled organ entombed within a pillar of the church. It can still be viewed behind a glass panel inside St. Mary's today.

THE TALBOT HOTEL
Oundle, Northamptonshire

Mary, Queen of Scots must have possessed one of the most psychically charged personas to ever drift across the pages of history. There is hardly a castle or house that she visited—as well as several that she didn't—that is not now haunted by her tragic shade. The place where you would expect to encounter her wraith is, of course, Fotheringay Castle, where she was beheaded in the Great Hall on February 8, 1587. But the castle was demolished long ago, and all that remains on the site is a mound in the grounds of a farmhouse. Much of its stone was used for new buildings in the neighborhood, and many of its furnishings ended up at sundry other locations.

The Talbot Hotel was originally founded in 636, but was lavishly modernized in the 1600s. When Mary's son, James I, ordered that Fotheringay Castle was to be razed to the ground, the landlord of the Talbot, William Whitwell, saw an opportunity to refurbish his hostelry in grand style at reasonable cost, and purchased many of the fixtures and fittings, including the great horn-windows. Whitwell also purchased the staircase down which the queen had walked to her execution, and with it, at no extra cost, came Mary's ghost.

On the polished wood of the balustrade, one can still see the imprint of a crown which, local tradition maintains, was left by the ring on Mary's finger as she held it on her way to the block. Less obtrusive is the psychic imprint of her restless wraith, which has been encountered by many guests. Some complain of a feeling of chilling unease as they descend the stairs. In one of the guest rooms, a woman lying in bed one night suddenly felt a weight pressing upon the covers. Attempting to reach for the light switch, she found herself unable to move as a clammy presence held her firmly against the bed. An unseen hand sometimes moves furniture around, and a picture that depicts Mary's execution has been known to suddenly jump off the wall. Guests crossing the outside yard have seen the ghostly face of a woman staring down from the horn-windows that came from Fotheringay.

Of course, the claims that it is Mary, Queen of Scots who haunts the Talbot are little more than speculation, and some even cast doubt on the authenticity of the staircase itself. There is, however, a direct physical connection between the tragic queen and the ancient hostelry. On the night before Mary was beheaded, the executioner lodged at the Talbot Inn where, it is recorded, he "partook of pigeon pie, drank a quart of best ale, and made a merry discourse with the serving girl till an early hour of the morning."

ABOVE: The Talbot Inn's historic staircase, which supposedly came from nearby Fotheringay Castle in 1628, is said to have been the staircase that Mary, Queen of Scots walked down to her execution in 1587.

BELOW: The heart of vicar John Styles can be seen behind this glass panel in a column of St. Mary's Church,

THE BELPER ARMS
Newton Burgoland, Leicestershire
❀ ❀ ❀ ❀ ❀ ❀ ❀ ❀ ❀ ❀ ❀ ❀ ❀ ❀ ❀ ❀ ❀ ❀ ❀ ❀

This attractive hostelry, parts of which are thought to be more than seven hundred years old, is the haunt of an unseen phantom of regular habits and malicious intent. The pub was built to provide accommodation for the stonemasons working on the village church and, although an extension was added in around 1700, the ghost seems to prefer the older sections of the inn. Because he always makes his presence known at five minutes to 4 o'clock, either in the morning or the afternoon, he has been nicknamed "Five-to-Four Fred," and a sure sign of his approach is a sudden drop in temperature. What happens next depends on the gender of the humble recipient of his ghostly touch. If female, the person can expect to feel his cold caress gently stroking her face; if male, then he will feel a pair of cold and clammy hands grasp his face as an unseen assailant attempts to suffocate him. Nor is Fred an adherent to the principles of political correctness, for many female staff have also been subjected to the indignity of a ghostly slap on the bottom as they go about their duties.

BOSWORTH HALL HOTEL
Husbands Bosworth, Leicestershire
❀ ❀ ❀ ❀ ❀ ❀ ❀ ❀ ❀ ❀ ❀ ❀ ❀ ❀ ❀ ❀ ❀ ❀ ❀ ❀

Bosworth Hall, with its rambling corridors, twisting staircases, and snug rooms, has a long history of religious strife. A Catholic stronghold for more than three hundred years it is, ironically, haunted by a Protestant ghost, yet a potent relic of its Papist past is still proudly displayed inside what is now a delightful hotel.

During the days when Oliver Cromwell ruled as Lord Protector of England and "Popery" was outlawed, the owners of the hall, the Maxwell family, who were devoutly Catholic, were attending a secret mass in the Chapel Room, when word arrived that a band of Roundhead troops was approaching the building. In a well-rehearsed routine, the priest made a dash for one of the many hiding holes that still riddle the building today, but either knocked over the chalice, spilling the communion wine, or cut himself, depending on which version of the tale you wish to believe. Either way, the stain has remained damp to the touch for nearly three hundred years, a curious enigma that defies explanation.

In 1881, the staunchly Protestant Lady Lisgar married the head of the family, Sir Francis Fortescue-Turvile, and came to live at Bosworth Hall. She made numerous alterations to the property, but is chiefly remembered for an infamous act of spiteful bigotry. When a Catholic servant lay dying, she refused point-blank to allow a priest into the house to administer the last rites. As a result, Lady Lisgar's ghost has been condemned to roam the corridors and rooms of the hall. Her spirit has been seen on staircases and in corridors—a silent, remorseful, and almost translucent shade, for whom there can be no escape from her eternal penance, which was incurred as a result of one uncharitable act.

ST. MARY-THE-VIRGIN
Bottesford, Leicestershire
❀ ❀ ❀ ❀ ❀ ❀ ❀ ❀ ❀ ❀ ❀ ❀ ❀ ❀ ❀ ❀ ❀ ❀ ❀ ❀

The church at Bottesford has long associations with nearby Belvoir Castle, many of whose occupants are buried here. The tomb of Francis, sixth Earl of Rutland, is of particular supernatural interest, since it is often called the "witchcraft tomb."

Francis lived at Belvoir Castle in the early years of the 17th century. Among the local people employed by his household were a Bottesford woman named Joan Flower, and her two daughters, Margaret and Phillipa. The Flowers were not a popular family, and Joan's neighbors considered her to be "monstrous and malicious." She was an unkempt woman with sunken eyes, who boasted of her atheism, consorted with familiar spirits, and reveled in the terror that her curses and oaths instilled in her neighbors. Few doubted that the three were witches, including the Countess Cecilia, who became increasingly suspicious of the family. When Margaret Flower was caught pilfering from the castle, the countess dismissed her on the spot, and in so doing

LEFT: The cozy bar of Newton Burgoland's Belper Arms is haunted by the ghost of "Five-to-Four Fred."

incurred the wrath of the Belvoir witches. The three women began casting spells on the Earl and his family. Soon afterward, both Francis and Cecilia suffered what were called "extra-ordinary convulsions."

Although the couple recovered, their eldest son, Henry Lord Roos, was stricken by a sudden illness and died. Then the couple's other son, Francis Lord Roos, was "most barbarously and inhumanely tortured by a strange sickness," and also died. Their daughter, Lady Katherine, was the next to feel the smart of the witches' revenge and was "set upon by their dangerous and devilish practices," although she recovered.

The final straw came when the Earl and Countess were again "brought into their snares" to keep them from having any more children. The three women were arrested and, while being examined by a Justice of the Peace, Joan Flower called for bread and butter, crying that she "wished it would never go through her if she were guilty." As she put the bread into her mouth, she mumbled a few words, and promptly choked to death. Her guilt was affirmed and, with it, the fate of her two daughters, who were hanged in Lincoln Jail on March 11, 1618.

"TWO SONS, BOTH WHO DIED IN THEIR INFANCY BY WICKED PRACTICE AND SORCERYE"

INSCRIPTION ON THE TOMB OF THE SIXTH EARL OF RUTLAND, BOTTESFORD

ABOVE: The red mark on the wrist of Dame Anne Smith in St. Michael's Church, Edmonthorpe, commemorates the night when this reputed witch turned herself into a cat.

Today, in the peaceful church of St. Mary-the-Virgin, an effigy of Francis, sixth Earl of Rutland, reclines, sandwiched between those of his first wife, Frances, and his second wife, Cecilia. His two sons kneel at the foot of the tomb, both holding skulls as symbols of their tragic deaths, while part of the inscription recalls how "In 1608 he married Lady Cecilia Hungerford, by whom he had two sons, both who died in their infancy by wicked practice and sorcerye."

ST. MICHAEL'S CHURCH
Edmonthorpe, Leicestershire

Inside the church in Edmonthorpe is the 17th-century tomb of Sir Roger Smith and his two wives. The lower effigy, that of Dame Anne Smith, who died in 1652, has a deep stain upon its wrist. This is said to commemorate the fact that this noble lady was in life a witch who, one night, turned herself into a cat to go about her nocturnal business. She was noticed by a butler, who promptly struck at her paw with a meat cleaver. When Dame Anne resumed her human form, an identical wound was visible upon her wrist.

THORNTON ABBEY
East Halton, Lincolnshire

❈❈❈❈❈❈❈❈❈❈❈❈❈❈❈❈❈❈❈❈❈❈

Remote and almost majestic in its sturdy elegance, the massive castellated gatehouse of Thornton Abbey stands as a proud and impressive testimonial to the skills of the ecclesiastical craftsmen who constructed it six hundred years ago. It is possessed of a compelling aura that casts a powerful spell as it towers over you, a threatening edifice of crumbling brown stone and hand-hewn brick, aloof, desolate, and thoroughly evil. Leering, sunken-eyed, stone faces, blackened by age, gaze down upon you as you pass beneath the abbey's exterior, their tongues poking out in devilish derision, while a bearded, demonic figure, its arms splayed in fiendish welcome, watches your progress like some silent guardian of a terrible secret.

The gatehouse, and the few scattered remnants of the abbey that lie beyond its rotting splintered gates, are reputed to be haunted by Thomas de Gretham, the fourteenth Abbot of Thornton. He was said to have been a practitioner of the black arts, a dabbler in witchcraft, and seeker after the pleasures of the flesh. His crimes were such that he was subjected to a particularly harsh and brutal punishment. Taken down to a dark room in the depths of the monastery, he was bricked up alive and left to die in the subterranean, airless dungeon. Little wonder that his sinister figure has been seen on several occasions, flitting around the grounds of Thornton Abbey, or staring with evil intent at surprised visitors who notice him standing in the shadowy corners of the towering gatehouse, where it is not difficult to imagine that all manner of dark forces are hard at work.

NEWSTEAD ABBEY
Ravenshead, Nottinghamshire

❈❈❈❈❈❈❈❈❈❈❈❈❈❈❈❈❈❈❈❈❈❈

George Gordon Noel Byron was born in London in 1788. His mother, Catherine Gordon, was a Scottish heiress, descended from James I of Scotland; his father, Captain "Mad Jack" Byron, was a decadent spendthrift, who squandered his wife's money and then abandoned both her and their newborn son when he fled to France to escape his creditors. Her husband gone, Catherine took her child to the family home in Aberdeen, where they lived frugally. Mad Jack died when Byron was three, and when Byron's great-uncle, William, died in 1798, the ten-year-old boy became the sixth Baron Byron and inherited the family's ancestral home, Newstead Abbey.

Henry II had founded Newstead Abbey in the 12th century in expiation for the murder of Thomas à Becket. It was home to a community of black Augustine Canons until its dissolution in 1539, when it was sold to Sir John Byron, who set

about building a magnificent residence alongside the abbey. There is an old belief that those who damage or deface a religious foundation will thereafter be plagued by bad luck, and the subsequent fortunes of Sir John's descendants would seem to provide ample confirmation of this theory. Poverty, scandal, family feuds, and childlessness blighted successive generations. William, the fifth lord, nicknamed "Devil Byron," refused to speak to his sister after she had become embroiled in a scandal. He would not even end the feud as she lay upon her deathbed, pleading for reconciliation. Her pathetic ghost is still said to wander the grounds wailing, "Speak to me my lord, do speak to me." Many believed that "Devil Byron" was insane, and his determined efforts to run down the house and grounds in order to ruin them for his heir certainly adds weight to this belief. As a result, the estate that ten-year-old George Gordon Byron inherited was rotten throughout. Damp came up through the floors, rain poured in through the roof, and the

only habitable part of the house was a small corner of the kitchen.

Byron didn't actually take up residence at Newstead until after his university days. He celebrated his arrival by throwing the first of his legendary parties, at which guests wore monk's robes and chased the serving maids through the cloisters in what, some of his detractors claimed, was little short of a sacrilegious orgy. A replica of the skull chalice, from which they drank communal wine, is still on display in the building.

Women adored Byron, and his affairs became the talk of polite society. There were even whispers of an improper relationship with his half-sister, Augusta Leigh, and when her daughter Medora was born, rumor was rife that Byron was the father. Byron's affair with the beautiful and tempestuous Lady Caroline Lamb, perhaps the most famous of his trysts, led to him being dubbed, by Lady Lamb herself, "mad, bad, and dangerous to know." It was, however, his marriage to Annabella

ABOVE: The former home of Lord Byron, Newstead Abbey, where a phantom monk keeps a menacing vigil and a "white lady" leaves a sweet scent in her ghostly wake.

Milbanke that, so he claimed, brought him into contact with Newstead's most famous ghostly inhabitant, the "Black Friar."

Today, a winding stone stairway leads the visitor to a sinister and stark little room, known as the Prior's Oratory, located next door to Byron's bedroom. Its scarred walls and wooden rafters exude an atmosphere that is nothing short of malicious, and the portrait of a friar that hangs upon the wall projects a menacing, almost threatening, aura. It is known to be a haunt of the abbey's Black Friar, whose appearance was seen as a fearsome harbinger that tragedy was about to befall the family. Byron swore that the Black Friar had appeared to him on the night before his wedding—but since he later described his marriage as the unhappiest event of his life, this may have been nothing more than poetic bitchery! However, the Prior's Oratory is one of the most chilling parts of the house, and several of the property's guides have suddenly been taken ill upon entering its ominous interior.

Mounting debt forced Byron to put Newstead Abbey up for sale, and the scandals of his personal life forced him to leave England in 1816, never to return. He died of rheumatic fever whilst fighting with the Greek freedom fighters in 1824. His body was brought back to England and was buried in the family vault at St. Mary Magdalene's church in Hucknall Torkard, near Newstead Abbey.

Today Byron's literary, if not literal, spirit dominates Newstead Abbey, and ghosts aplenty wander its wonderfully dark and atmospheric interior. The most persistent is a "white lady," whose appearance is always presaged by a sudden drop in temperature, and who leaves in her ghostly wake the distinctive and sweet smell of rose petals.

BELOW: The cavernous rooms and passages of Nottingham's Ye Olde Trip To Jerusalem, where ghostly footsteps have echoed down the centuries.

RUFFORD ABBEY
Ollerton, Nottinghamshire
❦❦❦❦❦❦❦❦❦❦❦❦❦❦❦❦❦❦❦❦❦

Rufford Abbey was built in 1148 for the Cistercian order, and for over four hundred years it thrived as a self-contained monastic foundation. But in 1536, during the dissolution of the monasteries, two Royal commissioners discovered that

the abbot, Thomas Doncaster, had several lady friends, both married and single, and that the monks had committed "disgraceful offenses." Rufford's days as a monastery were over, and it was granted to the powerful Talbot family, the Earls of Shrewsbury, who turned it into a magnificent country house. In 1626, it passed to the wealthy Savile family, one of whom—the eighth Baron, George Savile—was widely believed to have dabbled in black magic, and whose satanic practices are said to have sparked off the hauntings that afflicted Rufford Hall. One of the earliest records of sinister happenings can be found in the parish register of the nearby church at Edwinstowe, which records the burial of a man who "died of fright after seeing the Rufford ghost." In the days when it was a grand house, the servants would often comment on the apparition of a giant monk, whose fleshless skull would leer from beneath his dark cowl. Guests would report seeing his hideous figure reflected in the mirror as they sat at their dressing tables, while some ladies who stayed the night would often find their repose disturbed by the dreadful feeling of a cold, clammy baby snuggling up to them in bed!

Today, both the hall and the abbey stand in ruins amid the tranquil beauty of a country park. It is a cold and mysterious place, where graceful arches cast long shadows toward dark and sinister corners, and strange, ape-like stone creatures adorn the walls. The ghostly monk is still seen drifting around, while a "white lady" is said to glide around the

grounds and make the occasional foray into the buildings, where she melts away before speechless visitors.

YE OLDE TRIP TO JERUSALEM
Nottingham, Nottinghamshire

❧❧❧❧❧❧❧❧❧❧❧❧❧❧❧❧❧❧❧❧❧

The imposing sandstone crag on which Nottingham Castle stands is honeycombed by a network of caves, several of which are incorporated into what claims to be England's oldest pub, Ye Olde Trip to Jerusalem, established in 1189. A "trip" in those days was a place to rest and break your journey, and the unusual name comes from the fact that this old hostelry originally provided refreshment for Crusaders setting off for the Holy Land. It was through the inn in 1330 that Edward III entered Nottingham Castle when he came to arrest his mother's lover, Roger Mortimer, Earl of March, who had been responsible for the horrific murder of his father, Edward II, in 1327. Mortimer was captured in the Royal apartment and, ignoring the pleas of his mother, Isabella, to "have pity on the gentle Mortimer," Edward had him dragged to the Tower of London and executed at Tyburn. Isabella's pleadings are still said to sound from the depths of the rock, and footsteps are heard pacing around the caverns that form the pub's cellars, which can be visited with permission.

The pub's ancient rooms, which are little more than unadorned caves, are eerily atmospheric. The upstairs Rock Lounge, with its massive chimney, extending sixty or so feet up through the castle rock, is where one of the inn's most enigmatic and chilling relics is located. Encased in glass above the bar, there is a dust-caked model galleon. Until recently, it was suspended from the chimney, where it acquired its thick coating of dust and cobwebs over many decades, throughout which no one dared clean it. Only three people ever attempted the feat, and each one of them died shortly afterward. Convinced that there was a curse awaiting anyone who took a duster to the maritime model, successive landlords were content to

RIGHT: Was the uninvited guest (above) at the Freeman's Guild dinner in Coventry's Guildhall a ghost?

leave well enough alone. Until, that is, the unsuperstitious souls at the local environmental health department became alarmed by the detritus dropping into the drinks and meals of customers below and ordered its enclosure. Nervous of possible repercussions, the landlord called upon the services of a local medium, who attempted to exorcise whatever force might dwell within the model. Not long afterward, the lady was injured in an accident and spent several weeks in a coma.

ST. MARY'S GUILDHALL
Coventry, West Midlands

❧❧❧❧❧❧❧❧❧❧❧❧❧❧❧❧❧❧❧❧❧

Despite the spooky reputation of Coventry's Guildhall, no one thought to invite any of the ghosts to the Freeman's Guild dinner on January 22, 1985. Nonetheless, one of them seems to have dropped by unannounced, and to have taken up a position on the left top table, close to the Lord Mayor, Walter Brandish. No one sitting in the vicinity could remember him being there at any point during the dinner, but he is clearly visible in the photograph taken at the event.

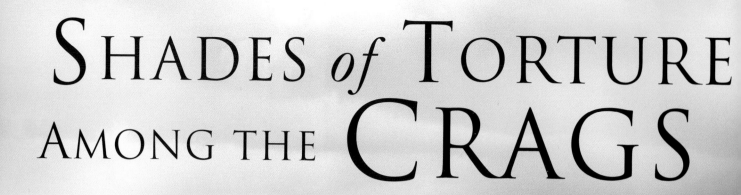

SHADES *of* TORTURE
AMONG THE CRAGS

And as the moon from some dark gate of cloud
   Throws o'er the sea a floating bridge of light,
Across whose trembling planks our fancies crowd,
   Into the realm of mystery and night, —

So from the world of spirits there descends
   A bridge of light, connecting it with this,
O'er whose unsteady floor, that sways and bends,
   Wander our thoughts above the dark abyss.

FROM *HAUNTED HOUSES*
BY HENRY WADSWORTH LONGFELLOW

DERBYSHIRE, STAFFORDSHIRE, CHESHIRE, & SHROPSHIRE

As the Industrial Revolution crept across the counties of Staffordshire, Cheshire, Derbyshire and Shropshire, coal and various other mineral deposits were mined from deep beneath the landscape, fuelling the expansion of the British Empire, while the chimneys above ground pumped their pollutants into the atmosphere. And yet within this industrial heartland is one of England's most fascinating landscapes, the Peak District. High, rocky crags rise from the rugged moorlands, while underground caverns and natural tunnels conceal a magical array of stalactites and stalagmites. It is a landscape that offers a wonderful variety of ghost lore and legend to anyone seeking England's mysteries.

KEY
1. Eyam
2. Longdendale
3. Mermaid's Pool
4. The Fauld Crater
5. Luds Church
6. St John's Church
7. Tamworth Castle
8. Capesthorne Hall
9. Image House
10. Lyme Park
11. Lilleshall Abbey
12. Wem Town Hall

EYAM
Derbyshire

The village of Eyam nestles in a sleepy hollow from which brooding hills climb steeply up to high moorland. It is a remote and isolated village, where poignant reminders of a long-ago tragedy are either scattered around the gardens, displayed upon the walls of the pretty stone cottages, or else lie forgotten in nearby fields.

PREVIOUS PAGES: Wild and rugged moorland straddles Kinder Scout, the highest mountain in the Peak District.

Next door to the village church stand several houses that share the collective name of "Plague Cottages." In September 1665, a tailor named George Vicars, who was lodging in one of the houses, received a parcel of damp cloth from London, which he spread out to dry before the fire. Unbeknown to him, he released into the village plague-carrying fleas, whose bite would, over the next twelve months, decimate the small community. Vicars himself was the first victim, and he was closely followed by his landlady's son, Edward Cooper. By October the pestilence was raging and, under the leadership of their vicar, William Mompesson, the residents of Eyam made the brave decision to cut themselves off from the outside world, in order to prevent the contagion from spreading throughout the district. Supplies were left at a well on the outskirts of the village that is known today as "Mompesson's Well," the stones of which still bear the hollows where payment was placed in pools of vinegar to purify the tainted currency. The church was closed, and families buried their dead in their own gardens or in surrounding fields; the eerie monuments marking the graves are still visible around the village today. By the time the last victim died on November 1, 1666, the outbreak had claimed the lives of 260 people out of a population of 350.

Today, Eyam does not morbidly dwell on its past, and only the memorial plaques on the cottage walls listing the names of those who died there, and the weathered tombstones strewn about the village, act as lasting reminders of the tragic events. But a strange aura of sorrowful stillness hangs over many of the buildings, several of which are said to be haunted.

A ghostly old man haunts the upstairs rooms of 17th-century Eyam Hall. Several ghosts haunt the Miner's Arms pub, including an elderly woman in a black bonnet, black cape, and black boots, thought to be a former landlord's wife, who was murdered in the 17th century. The pub, which was rebuilt in 1630 after the previous building had been destroyed by fire, is also haunted by two young girls, whom tradition has named Sarah and Emily, who lost their lives in the conflagration. Regulars in the bar have grown accustomed to their girlish footsteps skipping across the floors of the upstairs rooms. Guests spending a night at the pub have sometimes complained of their respite being disturbed by ghostly pranks, such as their bedroom doors opening and closing. This irritating activity appears to cause its ghostly perpetrators much merriment, for it is always followed by a peal of girlish giggling echoing down the corridor outside.

LONGDENDALE
Near Glossop, Derbyshire

✀✀✀✀✀✀✀✀✀✀✀✀✀✀✀✀✀✀✀✀✀✀

Longdendale—the long valley—is a ten-mile stretch of bleak but awesomely beautiful countryside that has long enjoyed a sinister and ghostly reputation. It is a lonely place of haunting mystery, which Daniel Defoe called "the most desolate, wild, and abandoned country in England." Traversing its bleak sedges as the last rays of the day cast the eerie glow of twi-

ABOVE: Eyam's "Plague Cottage," where in 1665 George Vicars inadvertently released plague-carrying fleas upon the village and decimated its inhabitants.

light across its menacing slopes is to feel truly alone and vulnerable. It is easy to understand why, in recent years, it has been dubbed "The Haunted Valley."

At around ten o'clock on the night of March 24, 1997, two women, who had come to the high moors in the hope of catching a glimpse of the Hale-Bopp comet, were startled by the appearance of a low-flying plane in the sky above them. They watched as it passed overhead and disappeared round one of the peaks. At more or less the same time, a local farmer saw the aircraft come round the peak and dive toward him, flying so low that he instinctively ducked. Moments later, several other witnesses heard the sound of a plane crashing and saw an orange glow light up the sky. The emergency services immediately began to receive calls from concerned locals, reporting the disturbing news that an aircraft appeared to have crashed. Believing a major incident to have occurred, mountain rescue teams were scrambled and headed for the high moors in the hope of finding survivors. For fifteen hours, over a hundred people, plus a Royal Air Force helicopter, searched every square inch of moorland, but they found no trace of a crashed plane, and in the weeks that followed none was ever reported missing. Whatever the witnesses had seen had apparently vanished into thin air — the "Phantom Bomber" of Longdendale had returned.

On the high moors, such as Bleaklow, numerous wrecked planes litter the rugged terrain. They are the rusting remnants of more than fifty aircraft that crashed into the peaks during and after World War II. One such heap of twisted debris is all that remains of an American B29 plane that crashed in 1948, killing all thirteen members of the crew. It is said that the ghost of its pilot, Captain Landon P. Tanner, has been seen wandering among the wreckage. There is also speculation about whether this, and many other crashes, were caused by one of the area's strangest phenomena, the "Longdendale Lights."

These strange, flickering balls of blue flame were locally known as the "devil's bonfires" and were attributed to either fairy folk or evil witches, intent on luring the unwary away to become sacrificial victims. There are records of the mysterious Longdendale Lights as far back as the 16th century, and even today their source still manages to evade the sophisticated equipment of mountain rescue teams. In July 1998, all the residents at the nearby Youth Hostel witnessed a brilliant blue light suddenly illuminate the entire district, which was visible for more than three minutes. Drivers on a nearby highway have been known to mistake the lights for those of another vehicle driving too close behind. Concerned observers, believing the lights are the distress flares of lost or injured walkers, frequently call out the emergency services, all of whom have long grown accustomed to the flickering lights fading slowly away as they get closer to them. It has been suggested that the pilots of the crashed planes may have mistaken the lights for directional beacons and then followed the beam into the hillside, on which the rusting piles of scattered and twisted metal now lie as eerie memorials to the long-dead aircrews.

On Thursday July 22, 1954, two Sabre 4 planes disappeared over the Peak District. The crashed fighters were discovered the following Sunday by two ramblers, who alerted the emergency services. The bodies of the unfortunate pilots were recovered, although the wreckage was left strewn where it had fallen. The cause of the crash was never officially established. Both planes were brand-new, and the pilots experienced fliers. However, the cockpit transmissions between them provide a tantalizing clue as to a possible cause of the crash. It is evident they were flying in low cloud and had become disoriented. "Where are we?" asked one pilot. "I'm not sure," came the reply. And then, apparently spotting a third aircraft, the second pilot gave the fatal order, "Just follow the other jet through the cloud." Those were the last recorded words between the pilots and, since no other planes were known to be flying in the area at the time, many people wonder if they were, perhaps, lured to their deaths by the appearance of the Phantom Bomber.

LEFT AND BELOW: The ghost of its American pilot, Captain Landon P. Tanner, haunts the rusting wreckage of his B29 plane that crashed into the peaks in 1948.

Mermaid's Pool
Kinder Scout, Hayfield, Derbyshire

❋❋❋❋❋❋❋❋❋❋❋❋❋❋❋❋❋❋❋❋❋❋

The pretty Peak District village of Hayfield possesses a fairly ordinary church where, in 1754, an extraordinary event occurred. On the last day of August, according to a contemporary account, a communal grave in the churchyard suddenly opened and hundreds of bodies rose from their coffins. "Singing in Consert," they began to ascend heavenward "to the great astonishment and Terror of several spectators." They left in their wake a "fragrant and delicious odor" and one of the Peak District's most abiding mysteries as to just what happened on that long-ago day.

A little way from the village, wild and rugged moorland straddles the lower slopes of the region's highest peak, Kinder Scout. It has been suggested that "kinder" may be a Celtic derivation of the Germanic "kunder," meaning either creature or prodigy. In a shallow ravine on the mountain's higher slopes, there is a dark and melancholic little pool, ringed by squelching bog, in the depths of which is said to dwell a mermaid, who may be the "creature" to

"To the great astonishment and terror of several spectators"

OBSERVER OF THE BODIES ASCENDING FROM A COMMUNAL GRAVE IN HAYFIELD IN 1754

ABOVE: Not even modern technology can explain the strange phenomenon of Longdendale's phantom lights.

whom the name refers.

It is a pool of lifeless marsh water exuding an aura of stark desolation. No animals come to drink from it, and no fish swim in its murky depths. The Celts believed that pools such as this were portals to the other world, and there is evidence to suggest that human sacrifices were carried out here, in order to placate the spirits that dwelt beneath and beyond its leaden waters. From this belief has evolved the legend of the mermaid, who lives deep beneath the sullen surface, and who can only be seen at midnight on Easter eve at. Those who undertake the exhausting journey to the pool at the witching hour on the given day will see the mermaid swimming toward them. Breaking the surface, she will stretch forth an ice-cold hand and either bestow upon you the gift of eternal life, or else drag you into the bottomless depths of her pool.

THE FAULD CRATER
Near Hanbury, Staffordshire

❋❋❋❋❋❋❋❋❋❋❋❋❋❋❋❋❋❋❋❋❋❋❋

At 11.11 a.m. on Monday, November 27, 1944, seismographs in both Geneva and Rome registered a massive eruption somewhere in Northern Europe. The source of the blast turned out to be the Fauld gypsum mines, where 3,500 tons of stored bombs and ammunition had ignited in what was the largest single explosion of the war before the dropping of the atom bombs onto Hiroshima and Nagasaki. A million tons of soil had been thrown eleven miles into the air, where it rained back down, showering an immense area of one square mile with thick, black sludge.

A huge bomb crater, a quarter of a mile in diameter and 300 feet deep, had been gouged out of the earth, and the reservoir on the hill above the village had burst, sending a 15-foot wall of mud surging into the Fauld plaster works. Two farms had disappeared from the face of the earth, pieces of dead cattle littered the landscape, and seventy people lay dead.

The crater still exists, and a feeling of total desolation exudes from it. Many visitors to the site have been overcome with a feeling of utter grief, while others have heard heartrending sobs echoing from deep beneath the ground, or have been startled by a disembodied, tuneless voice that sounds eerily in the air around them.

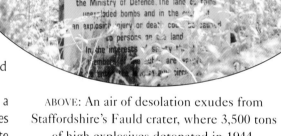

ABOVE: An air of desolation exudes from Staffordshire's Fauld crater, where 3,500 tons of high explosives detonated in 1944.

LUDS CHURCH
Gradbach, Staffordshire

❋❋❋❋❋❋❋❋❋❋❋❋❋❋❋❋❋❋❋❋❋❋❋

This damp, narrow, and secluded chasm, its sheer walls lined with fern and moss, has a long-held reputation for being haunted. Although both Robin Hood and Friar Tuck are reputed to have hidden here in their flight from the authorities, the ghost of this fearsome ravine is that of a girl who is supposed to have died under tragic circumstances in the early years of the 15th century. This hard-to-find spot was once used as a place of worship by the heretical followers of

the preacher John Wyclif, known as Lollards. The constant threat of execution forced the Lollards to hold their services in hideouts such as this, and its name is derived from a Lollard leader named Walter de Lud Auk.

One day, as Walter led fourteen of his followers, including his granddaughter Alice, in a service, their enthusiastic singing was heard by a passing band of soldiers. Approaching the cleft in the rocks that forms the entrance, the soldiers called upon the worshipers to surrender. Instinctively, the Lollards reached for their swords, whereupon one of the soldiers fired an arrow, which sped into the cavern, struck young Alice de Lud Auk, and killed her instantly.

The crestfallen Lollards sang a mournful hymn as they buried Alice at the entrance to the gully, and then surrendered to the soldiers. Walter died in prison, still mourning his beloved granddaughter, whose sad and silent ghost now haunts the spot where the tragedy occurred. She has been glimpsed hovering over the spot where her mortal remains are said to be buried. Should anyone move towards her she dissolves into the air, leaving behind bemused—and often terrified—witnesses.

ST. JOHN'S CHURCH
Burslem, Staffordshire

❋❋❋❋❋❋❋❋❋❋❋❋❋❋❋❋❋❋❋❋❋❋❋

In St. John's churchyard stands the tomb of Molly Leigh (1685–1748) which, contrary to normal practice, lies north to south, as opposed to the usual Christian direction of east to west. In Molly's day, the district around Burslem was a picturesque area of remote and scattered villages separated by green fields and rough lanes. The population of miners, potters, and farmers had little respect for religion and little need of education, and were more than content to while away their free time drinking and gambling. Dr. Plot, who arrived in the district toward the end of the 17th century, described its residents, unflatteringly, as "Moorland cheats" and the region in general as "impossible to get into and almost as impossible to get out of." But there was one thing that the rough-and-ready locals genuinely feared—the power of one possessed of the evil eye. It was a well-known fact that just one glance from such a person could bewitch humans, kill cattle, cause crops to fail, and inflict numerous untold horrors upon the district. All over Britain, people wore charms and amulets as protection against the baleful influence of "overlooking." People born with eye infirmities, such as casts or squints, were likely to be regarded as particularly dangerous, and their neighbors could be counted upon to make their lives utterly miserable.

Molly Leigh was just such a person. She was ugly and peculiar from birth, and her strange-looking eyes were blamed for children's illnesses and cattle's afflictions. Molly lived alone in a tiny cottage in the nearby district known as the Hamil. She kept as a pet an evil-looking black raven that would observe passersby in a sinister, unnerving manner. Children shunned Molly, parents played up to her, and the authorities left her well alone. She died in March 1748 and, as was the custom of the time, she was buried at night in the churchyard of St. John's. Molly's grave was positioned on a north–south axis, as it was believed that this would prevent her spirit from wandering.

After the funeral, the mourners, led by Parson Spencer, headed for Molly's cottage to bless it. It was a cold, damp night, and they had first fortified themselves with hot punch at the Turk's Head pub. As Parson Spencer pushed open the door, he suddenly jumped back in fright. Moments later he was running for all he was worth back to Burslem, the other mourners hot on his heels. Catching his breath, he told how he had seen the ghost of Molly Leigh, rocking to and fro by her fireside. The whole district was panic-stricken. A live witch had been bad enough, but the ghost of one was just too much to contemplate! There was only one thing for it. An exorcism would have to be performed.

And so it was that one evening at midnight, Parson Spencer, accompanied by three other vicars from neighboring parishes, approached Molly Leigh's grave, where they nervously exhumed her coffin. No sooner had they done so than they heard the dismal croak of a raven, and her sinister familiar flew down and perched upon the grave. The three neighboring clergymen fled in terror, but Spencer was determined to lay the

ABOVE: It was once believed that witches kept familiars in the form of animals, who aided them in their sinister rituals.

ghost once and for all. He caught the dreaded bird and, lifting the coffin lid, reunited it with the remains of its owner. The ordeal ended, he headed over to Molly Leigh's cottage and there prayed that she would trouble the district no more.

For many years afterward, children would dare one another to run three times around her grave, chanting "Molly Leigh, follow me into all the holes I see," whereupon they were assured that her spirit would rise from the grave and chase them from the churchyard.

BELOW: The tomb of Molly Leigh, Burslem's feared witch. It faces north-south to keep her soul from wandering around the district.

TAMWORTH CASTLE
Tamworth, Staffordshire

❈❈❈❈❈❈❈❈❈❈❈❈❈❈❈❈❈❈❈❈❈

Alfred the Great's daughter, Aethelfleda, who ruled Mercia between 899 and 918, raised the great mound on which Tamworth Castle was built in 913. Following the Norman Conquest, William the Conqueror gave the site to his supporter Robert de Marmion, who set about building the great keep and curtain walls that survive today. He also proceeded to expel the nuns from the nearby convent at Polesworth, an act that incurred the spectral displeasure of St. Editha, its founder, who appeared one night at his bedside and threatened him with a violent and untimely death if he didn't allow the nuns to return to their rightful home. To emphasize the point, she smote him across the head with her crosier, causing blood to flow from the resultant wound. The admonishing apparition so terrified de Marmion that he quickly restored all the confiscated lands to the nuns.

The middle room of the Norman tower is where de Marmion reputedly met with the fearful sister of "little mercy," and in commemoration of the ghastly occurrence it is today known as the "Ghost Room." The spectral nun has appeared

ABOVE: A vengeful nun is said to haunt Tamworth Castle in Staffordshire.

OPPOSITE, BELOW: Spectral beings often cross paths with the living at Capesthorne Hall.

to several startled witnesses here and, on account of the color of her habit, is known as the "Black Lady of Tamworth." Whether it is she who is behind the strange phenomenon that plagues other parts of the castle is uncertain. Many people have been disturbed by the sound of phantom footsteps descending the stairway, or by the low murmur of ghostly voices chattering from inside empty rooms; others have been startled to hear heavy furniture scraping across the floor of the Ferrers Room, pushed by a spectral, invisible hand.

CAPESTHORNE HALL
Monks Heath, Cheshire

❈❈❈❈❈❈❈❈❈❈❈❈❈❈❈❈❈❈❈❈❈

The Jodrell Bank satellite dishes, in all their gleaming white modernity, make bizarre neighbors for this imposing stately home of magnificent red brick, which is thought to have been designed in 1722 by John Wood, the famed architect who was behind the transformation of Bath into the most fashionable city of Georgian times.

The hall possesses several phantoms, whose spectral paths often cross over with those of the living residents. There is the ghostly procession of "writhing gray figures," that has been seen descending into a vault beneath the chapel. Occasionally, a mysterious "gray lady" has been known to flit around the corridors and cubbyholes of the atmospheric old house, much to the consternation of those who encounter her drifting shade.

However, the most bizarre apparition must be that observed by a member of the family, one dark, stormy night in 1958, when he was woken by the sound of his bedroom window noisily rattling. Looking to see what was causing the disturbance, he was stunned to see a severed arm that was attempting to open the window from the outside. Leaping from his bed, he raced over to the window and reached for the latch, but in the very moment he touched it, the spectral limb vanished into thin air.

ABOVE: A stone face, one of several carved on Image House by a convicted poacher, in the hopes of exacting revenge on the officials who were responsible for his apprehension and punishment.

Image House

Bunbury, Cheshire

There was a time when people were only too happy to settle their differences, or seek diabolical revenge, by using "sympathetic" or "image" magic. Today this is better known as voodoo, and is often associated with people sticking long needles into wax effigies of those who have offended them. The weathered stone images that adorn the walls of Bunbury's Image House are a vivid reminder of the days when any form of effigy would do. Each carving is thought to represent the officials responsible for sentencing a poacher to transportation in the 18th century. On his release and subsequent return to England, the vengeful poacher is said to have created these impressive stone reliefs of his punishers, and spent the remainder of his life heaping all manner of diabolical curses upon the figures, in the hope that his malevolent wishes would be visited upon their real-life counterparts!

LYME PARK
Disley, Cheshire

❦❦❦❦❦❦❦❦❦❦❦❦❦❦❦❦❦❦❦❦❦❦

A weathered weariness exudes from the brown-gray sandstone walls of this palatial stately home's dreary exterior. Yet, upon entering the house, you find yourself wandering a cozy labyrinth of dark passages and immense rooms hung with impressive tapestries resplendent with Grinling Gibbons' carvings and numerous secret panels.

For six hundred years, from 1346 to 1946, it was home to the Legh family, an early member of which, Sir Piers Legh, died in Paris in 1422 while fighting for king and country. His body was brought back to Lyme Park, where his grief-stricken widow, Lady Joan, watched the cortege wend its way along the drive to the spot where her husband was buried, thereafter known as "Knight's Low" or "Knight's Sorrow."

But, unnoticed in the cortege, was Piers's mistress Blanche who, following his interment, made her way to the nearby banks of the River Bolin and pined to death. When her body was discovered, it was buried on the spot, and the meadow was known thereafter as "Lady's Grave." But on stormy nights, when the clouds move eerily across the face of the moon and the wind races noisily through the trees of the park, a ghostly cortege is seen moving slowly along the driveway, followed by the howling figure of Blanche, her mournful cries sounding through the tempest, as she follows her lover to his final resting place time and time again.

The house's magnificent Long Gallery leads to the Knight's Bedroom which, on account of the fact it is haunted, is more commonly known as the "Ghost Room." There is a tradition that Mary, Queen of Scots slept in the room while a prisoner of Elizabeth I. It is a dark room that is dominated by a huge four-poster bed, upon which are carved strange, twisted, almost demonic faces.

Visitors have often complained of a sudden drop in temperature, or have come away puzzled by the sweet, ghostly smell of oranges that seems to pervade the air from time to time. A young boy visiting the room in 1999 became quite hysterical and started pointing at the bed, insisting that he could see a group of children playing on it, although the adults in the room could see nothing.

OPPOSITE: A huge four-poster bed dominates Lyme Park's "Ghost Room," where Mary, Queen of Scots is reputed to have slept.

BELOW: Did Tony O'Rahilly photograph a phantom girl in the flames when Wem Town Hall caught fire in 1995?

LILLESHALL ABBEY
Lilleshall, Shropshire

❦❦❦❦❦❦❦❦❦❦❦❦❦❦❦❦❦❦❦❦❦❦

The extensive and evocative ruins of this Augustinian abbey, dating from the 12th and 13th centuries, bask on peaceful green lawns beneath ancient yew trees. Dark, winding staircases spiral their way upward to crumbling parapets that afford stunning views across the surrounding countryside. But the peaceful tranquillity of this lonely place is sometimes shattered on bright summer evenings by the horrendous sound of agonized screams, echoing from deep within its foundations. They have been described as the sounds of someone being horribly tortured, and all who hear the screams agree that their terrifying intensity sends shivers racing down their spines.

WEM TOWN HALL
Wem, Shropshire

❦❦❦❦❦❦❦❦❦❦❦❦❦❦❦❦

On November 19, 1995, Tony O'Rahilly took a photograph of a fire at Wem Town Hall, and was astonished by the appearance of what appears to be a ghostly girl standing in the burning building. It has been suggested that she may be connected with a fire that devastated Wem in 1677, which was caused by a young girl accidentally setting fire to a thatched roof with a candle.

MYSTERIOUS MOUNTAINS *of* LEGEND

O 'tis a fearful thing to be no more;
Or if to be, to wander after death;
To walk as Spirits do, in Brakes all day;
And when the darkness comes, to glide
in paths
That lead to graves: and in the silent
Vault,
Where lyes your own pale shrowd, to
hover o'er it,
Striving to enter your forbidden Corps;
And often, often, vainly breathe your
Ghost
Into your lifeless lips.

FROM *OEDIPUS*

BY JOHN DRYDEN AND NATHANIEL LEE

WALES

Through centuries of political oppression, the Welsh imagination remained unvanquished, its roots buried so deeply in the Celtic past that no invader could ever destroy it. The poets, singers, and storytellers had an abundance of valiant heroes, beautiful maidens, and treacherous villains to inspire them. Even today, the remote, brooding peaks, deep forests, weather-beaten coastlines, and dark, sinister lakes still have the power to stir the spirit and unfetter the mind. It is a land where legends abound, and where oral tradition has ensured that the deeds of the past are never forgotten; as far as the Welsh are concerned, Wales was, is, and always will be, *hen wlad fy nhadau*, "land of my fathers."

KEY

1. St Govan's Chapel
2. Plas Mawr
3. Devil's Bridge
4. The Robber's Grave
5. The Skirrid Inn
6. Castell Coch
7. Aberglasney House and Gardens
8. The Boathouse

ST. GOVAN'S CHAPEL
Bosherston, Pembrokeshire

❈❈❈❈❈❈❈❈❈❈❈❈❈❈❈❈❈❈❈❈❈

Perched on a craggy chasm on the spectacular Pembrokeshire coast, this tiny chapel dates mostly from the 13th century, although parts of it are possibly as much as seven hundred years older. It is reached via a stone stairway of between sixty and seventy steps—the variance, legend tells us, is caused by the fact that it is impossible to count them

PREVIOUS PAGES: The 13th-century St. Govan's Chapel, once home to a saintly hermit.

accurately, as the number of steps differs according to whether you are ascending or descending.

St. Govan is believed to have been a 6th-century Irish monk who settled as a hermit in this tiny chapel beneath the remote, sea-sprayed rocks. A band of pirates once attempted to kidnap the cleric, but he was saved when a cleft in the rock miraculously opened and then closed behind him, to keep him safe until the danger had passed. It is said that if you make a wish while standing in this cleft, and turn around without changing your mind, your wish will be granted.

PLAS MAWR
Conwy

❧ ❧

It took twenty-one years to build this magnificent Elizabethan town house. Since its completion, no significant alterations have been made, and it remains much as it was when its first owner, Robert Wynne, occupied it in 1595.

The tragic events from which the haunting of the building evolved, however, took place at a later, though unspecified date. An owner of the house, so the story goes, went off to fight in a foreign war, leaving behind his pregnant wife and their young son. As the weeks rolled into months, the wife found his absence unbearable and became withdrawn. At length, however, she received word that her husband was coming home. Stirring from her melancholy, she took their young son and rushed to the top of the tower to await her husband's approach. They spent an uneventful day surveying the horizon and, as darkness fell, began the slow descent down the dark, dimly lit staircase. Moments later, the servants heard screaming and, rushing to investigate, found both the pregnant mistress and her young son unconscious at the bottom of the stairs. They were carried to a bed in the Lantern

BELOW: The lower of these three bridges is known as "Devil's Bridge" by virtue of the fact that it is reputed to have been built by Satan.

Room, and a young locum, Dr. Dic, was summoned to attend them. Nervously, he examined both mother and child before announcing that there was nothing he could do. Fearing their master's wrath, the servants fled the room and, locking the door behind them, left Dr. Dic alone with his dying patients.

That night, the master arrived home and, on hearing what had happened, rushed to the room. His wife and son lay dead upon the bed, but of Dr. Dic there was no trace. Cursing the locum, the master searched for him all night in a grief-stricken frenzy, and next morning he, too, collapsed and died. The good doctor was never seen again, and it has always been presumed that he had attempted to escape by climbing up the chimney, where his bones still lie in some long-forgotten nook. When the shadows of the night lengthen over Plas Mawr, the master's ghost is said to wander the house in search of Dr. Dic. Only when the unfortunate locum is given a proper burial will the master of Plas Mawr be freed from his onerous task. and pass over to be reunited with his wife and children.

DEVIL'S BRIDGE
Near Aberystwyth, Ceridigion

Set amid some of the most stunning scenery imaginable, Devil's Bridge is one of the most popular tourist attractions in Wales. The inevitable shops and cafeterias catering to the tourists, and the revolving iron turnstile through which you enter the gorge, detract a little from the mystery, but once you have made the perilous descent and craned your neck to look upward, your reaction will inevitably be one of sheer wonder. The foaming white waters of the rivers Mynach and Rheidol meet in a roaring crescendo of thunderous percussion as they crash into the gorge via a series of spectacular waterfalls. Sheer rock rises canyon-like from the boiling cauldron, and an abundance of plant life desperately clings to the dark walls. Spanning the whole breathtaking vista are three bridges precariously stacked on top of each other. The first, or bottom, one dates from the 12th century and is called Devil's Bridge, based on the legend that Satan was its builder.

Long ago, an old woman, out searching for her missing cow with her dog, was crestfallen when she found that the cow had somehow strayed to the other side of the gorge. She had all but given up hope of recovering the beast, when the devil appeared and offered to build her a bridge. His only condition was that he could claim for his own the first to cross over it. When the bridge had been built, the devil, anxious to claim his trophy, waited expectantly for the woman to cross over it. She was, however, a wily old lady and after taking a step forward, she produced a crust of bread and flung it across the bridge, whereupon her dog chased after it. After retrieving her cow, she thanked the devil for his assistance, bade him a warm farewell, and left him in eternal possession of a mangy old dog! The spot thereafter achieved a sinister reputation, and there is a local tradition that anyone crossing the bridge at night is in danger from a sinister ghoul that sneaks up behind them and hurls them into the raging waters below.

THE ROBBER'S GRAVE
Montgomery, Powys

❧❧❧❧❧❧❧❧❧❧❧❧❧❧❧❧❧❧❧❧❧❧❧❧

Montgomery is nominally a town although, in reality, it has more of a village feel to it. Its parish church, which is dedicated to St. Nicholas, boasts some impressive tombs within and a small cross outside, on which a simple inscription identifies it as "The Robber's Grave."

The cross marks the burial place of John Davies, "a melancholy, grief-haunted man," whose past was shrouded in mystery, but who in 1819 became the steward on the run-down farm owned by the widow Morris and her daughter, Jane. Thanks to his dedication, the fortunes of the business were soon reversed. But the sudden success angered a local man, Thomas Pearce, who had hoped to benefit from the widow's misfortune by acquiring the property at a bargain price. Davies' hard work had thwarted Pearce's ambitions and, as the resentment boiled within him, fortune intervened to seal the fate of the steward. Davies' hard work had earned him the respect of young Jane Morris. That respect soon turned to affection, and she abandoned her fiancé, Robert Parker, in favor of John Davies. Furious at the slight, Parker turned to Pearce, and the two men agreed that it would be in both their interests if they were rid of the troublesome steward for good.

Parker and Pearce duly carried out a violent robbery, leaving behind evidence implicating John Davies, who found himself charged with highway robbery. At Davies' trial, he was found guilty and sentenced to death. No sooner had the noose been placed around his neck than a fearful storm erupted. Rolls of thunder shook the town to its foundations. Lightning streaked across the sky, its bright flashes illuminating the rain-sodden face of the condemned man, whose voice rose above the tempest as

RIGHT: Until the 19th century, around 182 felons were executed inside The Skirrid Inn when it acted as the district's courthouse, and at least one of them still returns in disturbing ghostly form.

he turned to address the terror-stricken crowd, shouting, "If I am innocent, the grass, for one generation at least, will not cover my grave." As the trap fell, he spat a curse upon the two men whose evil machinations had brought him to his death, and called upon them to appear before God to account for their actions.

Parker died soon afterward, killed in a blasting accident. Pearce fared little better as he "wasted away from the earth." John Davies was buried in the simple grave where, as he had prophesied, no grass grew for many years. Even today, bare patches can still be seen upon it, and there is a belief that harm will befall anyone who attempts to tend the Robber's Grave.

THE SKIRRID INN
Llanfihangel, Powys

❧❧❧❧❧❧❧❧❧❧❧❧❧❧❧❧❧❧❧❧❧❧❧❧

The oldest reference to this delightful hostelry, nestling within the shadow of Skirrid Mountain, is in 1110, when John Crowther was sentenced to death for sheep stealing and was hanged from a beam inside the inn. Over the next eight hundred years, 182 felons would meet a similar fate, dangling by the neck over the building's stairwell. An unusual style of

> "IF I AM INNOCENT THE GRASS, FOR ONE GENERATION AT LEAST, WILL NOT COVER MY GRAVE."
>
> THE LAST WORDS OF JOHN DAVIES

customer relations, you may think, until you realize that, as well as serving up frothing tankards to thirsty travelers, the premises doubled as a courthouse. In the 19th century, the inn ceased to be a place for executions, and has since been a place purely dedicated to the sustenance of the living.

Needless to say, with such a sinister pedigree, The Skirrid Inn can offer many a ghostly tale to chill the blood. The spirits of those executed here often make their presences known in a rather direct and disturbing manner. Several people have felt the overwhelming sensation of an invisible

BELOW: The fairytale interior of Castell Coch, where a ghostly "white lady" still searches for her long-lost son.

noose being slipped around their necks and have been alarmed to feel it tightening. Although they always manage to break free from the malign grip, they bear the distinct impression of the rope marks on their neck for several days.

Another ghost to haunt the old and, in parts, spooky property is that of a woman who, although never seen, is both felt and heard by staff as she rustles past them, her progress marked by a distinct chill in the air.

In the 1990s, during a live radio broadcast from the inn, a medium who was asked for his impressions said that he sensed a young woman, possibly in her early thirties, who had died of consumption. Realizing that she had no way of proving or disproving the statement, the landlady thanked him politely for the information. Several months later, however, a couple researching their family history paid the landlady a visit. They told her that they were seeking information on one of their ancestors, Harry Price, who had owned the premises during the 18th century. They then revealed that his wife, Fanny Price, had died of consumption in her early thirties, and was buried in the local churchyard, where she still lies today.

CASTELL COCH
near Cardiff

With its lofty turrets and dramatic hillside location, Castell Coch is every bit the archetypal fairytale castle. The building that confronts the visitor today, however, dates only from 1870, when its pseudomedieval exterior and absolutely stunning interior were designed by the architect William Burges, for John Crichton Stuart, second Marquess of Bute. Since the Marquess was reputedly the wealthiest man in Britain, money was no object, and Burges was free to create a breathtaking palace that today stands as a vivid testimony to his vision and his patron's wealth.

The castle, however, stands on the site of a 13th-century fortress, which was little more than a moldering ruin for nearly two centuries before its amazing transformation. The ruins were the sad haunt of a ghostly "white lady," whose young son was said to have fallen into a bottomless pool of dark water somewhere within the castle precincts, and was never seen again. His grief-stricken mother never recovered from the tragedy and died of sorrow.

The lady's ghost was often seen walking amid its somber vestiges, a wretched figure whose eternal search for her missing son is still conducted through the sumptuous passages and corridors of the present building. There is a local rumor to the effect that Lady Bute, who continued to live in the castle after her husband's death, was driven away by the persistent and troublesome appearances of the ghost.

Aberglasney House and Gardens
Llangathen, Carmarthenshire

❧❧❧❧❧❧❧❧❧❧❧❧❧❧❧❧❧❧❧❧❧

One day in the 1630s, a housekeeper saw five disembodied candles floating around Aberglasney House's newly plastered "blue room," where the maidservants slept. The next morning, five maids were found dead in their beds. A charcoal stove left burning to speed up the drying of the plaster had asphyxiated them as they slept. Over the following centuries, the sinister "corpse candles" became one of Aberglasney's most abiding legends. Their fearsome flicker became renowned as a dreadful omen of approaching death, and one could be forgiven for thinking that the tragedy of the five maids had brought about a curse that has blighted the house ever since.

It was Anthony Rudd, Bishop of St. David's, who built Aberglasney House in the early 17th century. He intended it to be a family home for successive generations, but within a hundred years, mounting debts forced his descendants to put the estate on the market. Succeeding purchasers found that their family fortunes seldom fared better, as within two or three generations, they, too, would find themselves selling up and leaving.

As far as the house and grounds were concerned, however, the renovations and extensions carried out by various owners greatly enhanced the property. The Dyer family, owners between 1710 and 1798, added the magnificent Queen Anne facade; and a later owner, John Walters-Phillips, graced this with an aggrandized portico. The beautiful gardens were justly famous, and the row of yew trees, which was planted in the Middle Ages and later bent over to form an extended arch, is still wondered at today, just as it was in the 19th century.

At least one owner from the 19th century haunts the house. In 1803, Thomas Phillips, a wealthy surgeon serving with the East India Company, purchased Aberglasney House. Following his death in 1824, his amiable phantom was soon seen flitting around the house and grounds. Over the years, he appeared to gardeners, servants, and tradesmen, while more recently, guides at the property have reported that they have heard his ghostly footsteps.

BELOW: The medieval tunnel of yews at Aberglasney House, located in a "garden lost in time."

Following Thomas Phillips' death, successive owners found their lives blighted by ill luck. Children would die in infancy; couples with dynastic ambitions would remain childless; old and young alike would suddenly die, or find their fortunes, both monetary and spiritual, brought to the brink of ruin. An aura of melancholic decay descended upon the property, and by the end of the 1960s it had been abandoned. Weed and nettle crept over the magnificent gardens, while damp and rot chewed through the fabric of the house. Whatever nature left untouched, vandals were quick to destroy, and by the 1990s the place lay forgotten and derelict.

And then a miracle happened. A small band of enthusiasts, who had kept a concerned eye on Aberglasney's decline, formed a trust and, thanks to a wealthy American benefactor, were able to purchase the property. They rescued the gardens and halted the decay—but they also awakened the spirits of the past. The builders who set to work on the hollow shell of the old house often saw the wraith of a young girl standing

in a corner of the basement, apparently cooking. Guides, absorbing the atmosphere of the peaceful cloisters, would often be disturbed by the sound of footsteps behind them, only to find themselves quite alone when they turned round.

It is, however, in Pigeon House Wood, at the rear of the property, that the most disturbing phenomenon is experienced. There is a certain spot where many visitors sense a feeling of dreadful unease. It intensifies as they descend the earthen path until, at the edge of the wood, it is replaced by sudden fear, followed by an eerie coldness. A medium, visiting the property in 1999, said that she sensed someone trying to evade capture in the wood. The place in which people begin to feel uneasy, she explained, was where the fugitive's pursuers had spotted him. He made a desperate run for freedom, but was felled by a single bullet in the area where the sudden fear and coldness is most often felt.

Aberglasney is a gem, nestling amid some of the most stunning scenery imaginable. The sad aura that still hangs heavy over the house is in sharp contrast to the sheer beauty of its gardens. It is a tranquil place that has resigned itself to a ripe old age, and its sobriquet "a garden lost in time" is both deserved and accurate.

THE BOATHOUSE
Laugharne, Carmarthenshire

In the early hours of Wednesday, November 4, 1953, the poet and playwright Dylan Thomas returned to his room at the Chelsea Hotel in New York and uttered the legendary words, "I've had eighteen straight whiskeys. I think that's a record." Six days later—having slipped in and out of consciousness—he was dead, killed by what was poetically described as a "severe insult to the brain," but which most would call acute alcohol poisoning.

Dylan's body was returned to the town of Laugharne, and his coffin was placed on public display at his mother's house, The Pelican. Here, mourners who came to pay their last respects and raise the odd glass to his memory were allowed to lift the lid and view his body. On November 24, Dylan was buried in the local graveyard beneath a simple white cross, and the tiny Welsh town soon became a place of pilgrimage as admirers of all nationalities came to pay their respects and visit the

LEFT: The "seashaken house on a breakneck of rocks," where Dylan Thomas lived his last years, and to which his mother, Florence, still returns, much to the consternation of staff and visitors.

"seashaken house on a breakneck of rocks" that was Dylan's home for the last four years of his life.

Dylan and his wife Caitlin had moved into The Boathouse in the spring of 1949. It was a ramshackle, primitive building, and damp had stained the ceilings and made the woodwork spongy. The rats that scurried around the outside toilet often found their way into the house itself. Money, or the characteristic lack of it, was a constant worry, causing Dylan to wryly observe that he found himself "forever at debt's door."

In the tiny workshop, which still perches precariously over the edge of the cliff, Dylan gazed out across the tidal flats and sandbanks of the Taf Estuary and composed what is perhaps his best-known poem, "Do Not Go Gentle Into That Good Night." He also completed his "play for voices," *Under Milk Wood*, resurrecting a facetious Welsh place name, "Llareggub," that he had first used in *The Orchards*. Dylan's publishers had not thought to spell the name backward, and thus it successfully evaded their repeated attempts to censor his work!

Following Dylan's death, Caitlin would not stay at The Boathouse, so his mother, Mrs Florence Thomas, became the tenant, and it is her ghost that is thought to haunt the

ABOVE: The tiny workshop from which Dylan Thomas gazed out across the Taf Estuary and wrote his most famous poem, "Do Not Go Gentle Into That Good Night."

building. She is never seen, but rather makes her presence known in sundry other ways. Several staff have been surprised on opening the premises to hear the sound of a chair scraping over the upstairs floor, as though someone has risen briskly from the table to avoid them.

Lights, switched off at the end of the day, have been found on again the next morning, and on several occasions paintings have been removed from the walls overnight and placed carefully on the opposite side of the room. The psychically inclined have detected cold spots, most notably around the staircase, and mediums have sensed Florence's presence in the parlor, where she eventually died in 1958.

"I'VE HAD EIGHTEEN STRAIGHT WHISKEYS. I THINK THAT'S A RECORD."

DYLAN THOMAS, COMMEMORATING THE DRINKING BOUT THAT KILLED HIM

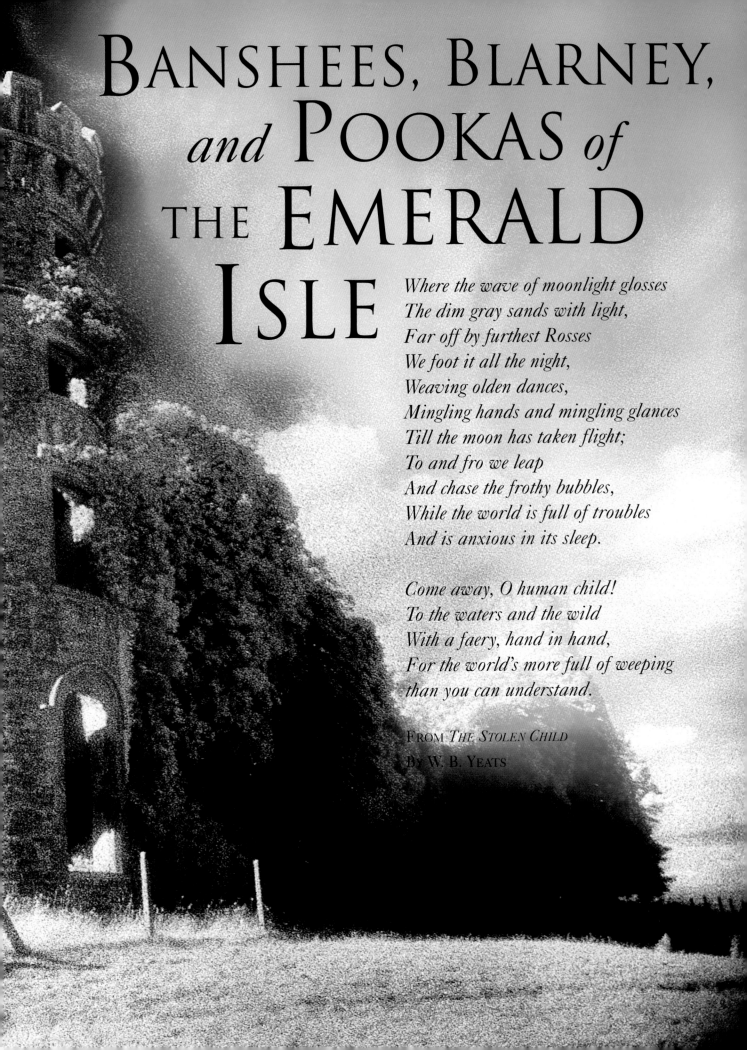

BANSHEES, BLARNEY, and POOKAS of THE EMERALD ISLE

Where the wave of moonlight glosses
The dim gray sands with light,
Far off by furthest Rosses
We foot it all the night,
Weaving olden dances,
Mingling hands and mingling glances
Till the moon has taken flight;
To and fro we leap
And chase the frothy bubbles,
While the world is full of troubles
And is anxious in its sleep.

Come away, O human child!
To the waters and the wild
With a faery, hand in hand,
For the world's more full of weeping
than you can understand.

FROM *THE STOLEN CHILD*
BY W. B. YEATS

IRELAND

From its deeply ingrained Gaelic roots, Ireland is blessed with an oral tradition that has survived centuries of political oppression and national calamity. It is a land of paradoxes—it is beautiful but bleak, mystical yet strangely modern, peaceful yet divided, rich in talent yet poor in resources. It is a land of storytellers, where you can be regaled with the most unbelievable tales and yet find yourself accepting them without question. There is mystery in the landscape of ruined castles, prehistoric stone circles, stately homes, and windswept wilderness. There are the legends of banshees, leprechauns, and the dreaded "pookas." All in all, Ireland fires the imagination yet calms the spirit, and to listen to people telling their ghost stories by a glowing peat fire in a traditional pub is a truly fantastical experience, in which fact matters little, and poetry is everything.

KEY
1. Ballynacarriga Castle
2. Charles Fort
3. Dùn an Òir
4. Thoor Ballylee
5. Leap Castle
6. Killakee House
7. Kilmainham Gaol
8. St Michan's Church
9. Killua Castle
10. Castle Leslie
11. Springhill
12. Dobbins Inn Hotel

PREVIOUS PAGES: Killua Castle, where a feeling of chilling melancholy emanates from the ivy-clad walls, and a ghost of uncertain gender wanders the timeworn interior.

OPPOSITE: Irish legend speaks of numerous untamed beasts that stalk the hours of darkness, intent on spiriting away unwary mortals.

BALLYNACARRIGA CASTLE
Dunmanway, Cork

❦❦❦❦❦❦❦❦❦❦❦❦❦❦❦❦❦❦❦❦❦❦

The Irish name of this four-story tower is Beal na Carraige, meaning "the mouth or passage of rock." It is perched upon a rocky prominence and overlooks the waters of Ballynacarriga Lough. An unusual feature of its crumbling interior is the number of important stone carvings that can be seen around the walls of what was once the third floor. On one window arch is a depiction of Christ on the cross together with two thieves, one on each side of him, while nearby are carved a crown of thorns, a hammer, and a heart pierced with two swords. One window contains the initials R. M. C. C. together with the date 1585. These are believed to be the initials of Randal Murlihy and his wife, Catharine Cullinane, plus the date when the building was erected. Opposite is the carved figure of a woman with five roses, which local tradition claims represents Catherine Cullinane and her five children—but which is more likely to depict the Blessed Virgin.

The roof and parapets of the castle were long ago removed by a garrison of Cromwellian troops who had occupied the fortress for a time and who, as was their custom, took down the overhanging parapets in order to render the building defenseless. But enough of the fortification remains to provide the visitor with a good impression of what it was like to live in a medieval castle. It was an age when belief in a darker side of nature had a firm grip on the imagination, and it was well known that harmful spirits roamed the night, intent on inflicting injury on humans that chanced to cross their path.

Built into the thickness of the second floor wall, there is a mural gallery which leads the intrepid visitor to the garderobe, or lavatory, which stands over a chute known as "Moll the Pooka's Hole." A "pooka" was the most feared of all the creatures that prowled the night. They were strange and thoroughly evil beings, with male heads and the bodies of goats, horses, or dogs. They could fly short distances, although they had no wings, were extremely ugly and ill-tempered, and were to be avoided at all costs. They ran in packs, and their sole desire was to inflict as much harm as possible upon defenseless humans. They caused crops to fail, children to suddenly die and, worst of all, stole newborn babies. Irish peasants would ascribe accidental falls to the malign influence of a pooka, and ruined or wrecked castles were often associated with them—the foul-smelling chute of a garderobe being the ideal portal by which these creatures could gain access and wreak their devilish mayhem upon the inhabitants.

CHARLES FORT
Kinsale, Cork

❀❀❀❀❀❀❀❀❀❀❀❀❀❀❀❀❀❀❀❀❀

Constructed in the late 17th century on the site of an earlier coastal fortification, this star-shaped fortress, with its five bastions and two surviving brick sentry boxes, straddles a sea-swept rocky trajectory. Not long after the completion of the fort, Colonel Warrender became its commanding officer. He was a strict authoritarian who believed in a rigorous regime of discipline, and had little sympathy for any man who stinted or faltered at his duties. His daughter, Wilful, a vivacious and beautiful girl, fell in love with Sir Trevor Ashurst, who was an officer at the fort, and the two were duly married. At sunset on the day of their wedding, the two were strolling along the battlements when the bride noticed some flowers growing on

BELOW: Charles Fort, where three tragic deaths on a long-ago wedding day have left an indelible mark on the monument's ethereal plain.

the rocks beneath, and commented on their beauty. A sentry agreed to climb down and pick the flowers for her on the condition that her husband would take his place on duty. Sir Trevor agreed, donned the soldier's greatcoat, took his musket, and entered the sentry box, while its original occupant began the perilous descent to the rocks below. It had been a long day, and no sooner had Ashurst sat down than he fell fast asleep. Just then, Colonel Warrender began his routine inspection of the fort's sentry boxes. He was furious to find a guardsman asleep on duty and, drawing his pistol, shot the man through the heart. As the sentry fell to the ground dead, his coat opened and the Colonel saw that he had killed his own son-in-law. When Wilful learnt of her husband's death she was inconsolable and, letting out a howl of despair, raced to the battlements, from which she threw herself to her death. The sight of his daughter's body proved too much for Colonel Warrender and, placing his pistol against his head, he pulled the trigger and blew out his brains.

Three tragic deaths on a day that should have been a celebration have, inevitably, left their mark upon the ether of this casemated, windswept monument. It is the ghost of Wilful

Warrender who haunts the garrison. Wearing a flowing white dress, she drifts in mournful despair, either around the ramparts or up and down the stairs of the stronghold. Those who encounter her silent wraith describe her as being very beautiful, but also very pale. She passes by them, her dark eyes fixed on some distant objective. She pays them no heed, and soldiers used to speak of their alarm at seeing her pass straight through locked doors, while others complained of being pushed down the stairs by an unseen hand, presumably hers.

DÙN AN ÒIR
(OR FORT DEL ORO)
Dingle Peninsula, Kerry

During the 16th century, Dingle became a significant trading port and developed very strong connections with Spain. On July 15, 1579, Charles V of Spain sent an expeditionary force to Dingle under the leadership of James Fitzmaurice-Fitzgerald, a cousin of the peninsula's powerful overlord, Gerat, sixteenth Earl of Desmond. Shortly after landing, Fitzmaurice-Fitzgerald was ambushed and killed in a skirmish with the Burkes of Limerick. Although the Earl of Desmond had promised to help his kinsman and his contingent, he was also anxious not to alienate Queen Elizabeth, so he sent word to her forces about the possible threat. The expedition resulted in failure for the Spanish, and after a few days they left Dingle and sailed round the coast, where they landed at Ferriters Cove. On the headland they built a fort, the Fort del Oro, or Dùn an Òir as it is known in Gaelic, as a base for operations against England. In November 1580 an English force, commanded by Lord Grey de Wilton, besieged the fort. The garrison had again hoped for promised assistance from the Earl of Desmond but none was sent, and finally the expeditionaries were battered into submission. When the Spanish set down their arms to surrender, the English troops massacred them in cold blood and either left their corpses in heaps, or cast them into the sea to be washed away. On the anniversary of the dreadful slaughter, people in the locality have often heard agonized voices crying in Spanish, and smelled the terrible stench of rotting flesh carried upon the breezes around this wild spot.

THOOR BALLYLEE
Gort, Galway

Once known as Islandmore Castle, this evocative and atmospheric stone tower, with its narrow, time-worn stairs, was a virtual ruin when the poet W. B. Yeats (1865–1939) purchased it in 1917 for the nominal sum of £35. Yeats renamed it Thoor (the Irish word for tower) Ballylee, commenting that, "I think the harsh sound of Thoor amends the softness of the rest." Following considerable restoration, the property was finally habitable in 1919, when it became Yeats's summer residence and, thereafter, a central symbol of his poetry. Yeats was a devotee of the occult, once observing that, "The mystical life is the center of all that I do and all that I think and all that I write." He believed implicitly in the existence of ghosts, and was convinced that the tower was haunted by an Anglo-Norman soldier. A later curator was also convinced that a spectral form wandered the worn stairway of the tower, and was reluctant to ascend it as the day turned into night. This feeling was evidently shared by her pet dog, who would show signs of terror at something it could apparently see in the downstairs rooms.

In 1989, an English family touring County Galway arrived at the tower one summer's afternoon just as it was closing. Since they wished to photograph Yeats's sitting room, the curator obligingly reopened the window shutters so that a picture could be taken. David Blinkthorne stayed alone in the room to take photographs while his family went off to explore the rest of the building. When the film was developed, Mr.

RIGHT: W.B. Yeats and his wife, Georgie, through whom he contacted the spirit world.

"I DECLARE THIS TOWER IS MY SYMBOL; I DECLARE/ THIS WINDING, GYRING, SPIRING TREAD-MILL OF A STAIR IS MY/ ANCESTRAL STAIR."

W.B. YEATS ON THOOR BALLYLEE, FROM "BLOOD AND THE MOON"

apparition. The ghostly boy's identity still remains a mystery, although some have suggested that he may have been Yeats's own son.

Blinkthorne was astonished to see a the figure of a short-haired young boy in one of the prints. No one else had been in the room when the photograph was taken, and none of the other prints showed the strange and inexplicable

LEAP CASTLE
Leap, Offaly

Nightmares, both real and imagined, abound around what is generally acknowledged to be Ireland's most haunted castle. Standing upon a vast throne of solid rock, it was once the stronghold of the O'Carrolls, and its eventful history is mostly written in their blood. In the 16th century, O'Carroll of Leap held a lavish banquet at the castle and invited a rural

BELOW: Thoor Ballylee, former home and central symbol to the mystical Irish poet W.B. Yeats.

branch of his own sept to partake of his hospitality. No sooner had the unfortunate guests sat down to dinner than he massacred every one of them. Inter-clan bloodshed was a common occurrence, and members of the tribe attended family get-togethers or reunions at their peril! In the "Bloody Chapel" above the main hall of the 14th-century tower, "one-eyed" Teige O'Carroll is said to have slain his own brother as he knelt in prayer at the altar. Since clan members held each other in such low esteem, it is not surprising that those outside the family circle could expect little mercy, and

BELOW: Leap Castle, former stronghold of the warring O'Carrolls and widely acknowledged as the most haunted castle in Ireland.

would often find themselves subjected to gruesome and barbaric treatment.

After the house had been destroyed by fire in 1922, three cartloads of human bones are supposed to have been removed from the dungeons beneath the castle. A glowing ethereal light has been seen shining from the window of the Bloody Chapel in the dead of night by those who happen to be driving by on a nearby road. Some people have complained of certain "spots" where a feeling of sheer evil hangs heavy in the air. Others have had alarming encounters with a lustrous lady wearing a billowing red gown, who suddenly comes towards her witnesses with arms wildly flailing—and then suddenly disappears, leaving a frosty chill in her menacing wake.

KILLAKEE HOUSE
Killakee, Dublin

❈ ❈ ❈ ❈ ❈ ❈ ❈ ❈ ❈ ❈ ❈ ❈ ❈ ❈

In 1968, Mrs. Margaret O'Brien and her husband, Nicholas, purchased what was then a derelict building, with the intent of turning it into an arts center. Several workmen lived on the site during renovation, and they soon grew accustomed to eerie sounds and uncanny happenings. But when a large feline mysteriously appeared before them and then suddenly vanished, the builders became decidedly uneasy, and the legend of "The Black Cat of Killakee" was born.

Mrs. O'Brien thought the stories were nonsense to begin with, but then she, too, saw the creature and, as she put it, "began to understand the fear." The first time she crossed its path it was squatting on the flagstones of the hallway, glaring at her. Every door in the house was locked both before and after its sudden appearance and subsequent disappearance.

The painter Tom McAssey had the most famous confrontation with the mysterious creature. In March 1968, he and two other men were working in a room of the house when the temperature began to drop alarmingly. Suddenly, the door swung wide open, and a hazy figure appeared in the darkness. Thinking it was someone playing a joke, Tom called out, "Come in, I can see you." All three men froze in terror when the reply was a low, angry growl. Moments

later they fled the room, slamming the door behind them. But, when Tom McAssey looked back, the door was again wide open, and a hideous black cat with blazing red eyes was snarling at him from the shadows of the room. "I thought my legs wouldn't take me away from the place," he later recalled, "I was really in a bad state." Following this chilling encounter, Margaret O'Brien had the building exorcised, and things quietened down for a time.

But in October 1969, a group of actors staying at the arts center decided to hold a séance, and the disturbances began again. Furthermore, they seemed to have raised the spirits of two nuns, who would appear before startled witnesses in the center's gallery. A local medium, Sheila St. Clair, visited the property and claimed that the phantoms were the unhappy spirits of two women who had assisted at satanic rituals held during the meetings of the "Hell Fire Club" in the 18th century. The Irish branch of this notorious club held its sinister assemblies in a hunting lodge, the ruins of which can still be seen on Montpelier Hill behind the house.

Local legend tells how Richard "Burnchapel" Whaley, a member of one of the area's richest families, had joined the club and had reveled in the debauched rituals. These are said to have included the burning alive of a black cat on at least one occasion, the worshiping of cats in place of Satan himself, the setting on fire of an unfortunate woman stuffed inside a barrel, plus the beating and murder of a poor, deformed boy. At a meeting of the club in 1740, a servant is said to have spilled a drink on Whaley, who was so enraged by

reminders still exist of its more sinister bygone days. Chief among these is Tom McAssey's portrait of "The Black Cat of Killakee" that gazes hauntingly down from one of the walls, its eerie red eyes and almost human features enough to send icy cold shivers racing up and down the spine.

KILMAINHAM JAIL
Dublin

❧❧❧❧❧❧❧❧❧❧❧❧❧

The vast and eerie Kilmainham Jail is Ireland's largest unoccupied prison. Its echoing corridors and poignant courtyards provide a vivid idea of what it would have been like to find yourself confined in one of these forbidding bastions between 1796, when it opened, and 1924, when it closed. As well as housing many common criminals, it was also the place where fourteen of the sixteen leaders of the republican insurrection, known as the Easter Rising, of April 1916 were detained and executed. A plaque in the jail's courtyard commemorates those patriotic men, who bravely and defiantly faced the firing squads in the cold early mornings of May 1916. The last to die was James Connolly, who had to be tied to a chair as he was unable to stand on his own, due to his terrible injuries.

ABOVE: Kilmainham Jail's chilling interior is the eerie haunt of an abundance of specters and strange phenomena.

the accident that he had the servant doused in brandy and set ablaze. The subsequent fire burned down the lodge, in the process killing several members of the club.

In July 1970, a dwarfish skeleton was discovered, buried beneath the kitchen floor of the building. In the grave with it was the brass statuette of a monstrous demon, which gave credence to at least the legend of the deformed boy. A priest was called to give the body a proper burial, and thereafter the manifestations of the black cat ceased.

Today, a pleasant restaurant occupies the old house, and hellish felines seem to be very much a thing of the past. But

With such an eventful, and often gruesome, history, it is inevitable that Kilmainham Jail should have several ghosts. The building had stood empty for many years before a dedicated band of volunteers set about restoring it in the early 1960s. At the time, the governor's quarters were being utilized as a home by a resident caretaker. Not in the least bit perturbed by the fact that his front windows looked out onto the place where the gallows had once stood, the man carried out his duties with cool, levelheaded efficiency. One evening, he was preparing for bed when he happened to glance from a side window and saw, to his surprise, that the chapel lights, which he had only just turned off, had been switched back on. He walked across to the chapel, switched off the lights, and returned home where he once more prepared to retire. But on looking from the window, he saw that the chapel lights were again blazing. He made the long, cold walk to the chapel a total of three times in that one night.

During the restoration yet another man, whom colleagues described as being "very religious and teetotal," was painting in the dungeon area of the prison, when a huge gust of wind suddenly blew him against a wall. Battling hard against the tempest, he managed to fight his way out of the dungeon, where his ashen face and shaking hands were vivid testimony to his terrifying brush with the uncanny force. He then refused point-blank to ever work in, or even set foot in, the jail again.

On yet another occasion, a volunteer was decorating the 1916 Corridor when he heard what he took to be a colleague's heavy footsteps climbing the stone stairs and walking along the passage behind him. Turning to greet whomever it was, he was astonished to find no one else in the corridor, despite the fact that the plodding footsteps continued, as though some invisible presence had just walked right past him.

Several children visiting the old jail have paused, terrified, on the threshold, refusing to go one step further, while one guide who was particularly susceptible to psychic sensations claimed that there was an evil and fearsome aura around the balcony of the chapel. Others, however, sense the jail to be a tranquil place, and speak fondly of how the eyes of the thousands of past inmates watch them, apparently looking out for their well-being.

Perhaps the last words on the haunting of the jai should go to the old caretaker, who was always pointing out that no one should ever fear the inmates, because they knew that those who now run the prison are only trying to tell their often forgotten stories: "But," he would say, "the soldiers and the guards? Now they're a different matter."

ABOVE: The execution yard at Kilmainham Jail, where leaders of the 1916 uprising bravely faced the firing squads.

OPPOSITE: These preserved cadavers in the vaults of St. Michan's Church appear to have just fallen asleep, and you find yourself expecting them to emit a loud snore at any moment.

ST. MICHAN'S CHURCH
Dublin

❧ ❧ ❧ ❧ ❧ ❧ ❧ ❧ ❧ ❧ ❧ ❧

St. Michan is thought to have been a Danish bishop who, in 1095, built a church above vaults that had been constructed upon the site of an ancient oak forest. The church was rebuilt in the 18th century and contains, among other things, the death mask of the charismatic Irish patriot, Theobald Wolfe Tone (1763–1798), and the organ on which Handel is reputed to have practiced his *Messiah* before the first performance in Dublin. The philosopher Edmund Burke was christened here, and the funeral of Home Rule leader Charles Stewart Parnell also took place here.

It is in the dark vaults beneath the church, however, that you will find one of the creepiest and most unique haunted locations in the whole of Ireland. You enter this subterranean world via two heavy iron doors that open onto a steep flight of stone steps, down which you descend into eerie darkness. The air, however, is strangely warm and fresh, not in the least like the cold and clammy atmosphere you would expect to find in such a place. As your eyes grow accustomed to the dark, you notice a series of vaulted cells that lead from a central passage. In several of the chambers, coffins are stacked in untidy piles as generations of the same family lie on top of one another. In places, the weight of the dead pressing upon the dead has resulted in the coffins collapsing into each other. In the past, arms, legs, or even heads would protrude from their final resting places, as if successive generations were posing for some grotesque and macabre family portrait.

What is even more remarkable is that, despite the fact that some of these people died 500 years ago, they have not crumbled into dust, but have been preserved like mummies, their flesh the texture of tanned leather. Even more bizarre, their joints are supple and can actually be moved! The only living creatures in this underground world of twisting shadows

are spiders. Their webs, woven thick across the ceilings and walls, form grim, gray veils that disappear into dark corners. In one vault, four open coffins display occupants whose heads are either thrown back or lying to one side, their mouths open as if they have just fallen asleep—and you find yourself expecting them to emit loud snores at any moment. The body of one man lies with one leg crossed over the other, the traditional posture denoting a crusader. Such is the state of preservation that you can actually examine the nails of someone who died around 800 years ago. There was a time when you could even stoop and shake his hand, but such intimacy is now forbidden, thanks to the accidental breaking of several of his fingers!

The remarkable preservation of the cadavers is thought to be the result of the air being chemically impregnated by the remains of the oak forest that stood on the site in ancient times. As long as the vaults remain dry, decay ceases. Let only a little moisture enter, and the bodies crumble into a fine dust. In 1853, brothers John and Henry Sheares, who were beheaded after being hanged in the 18th century, were recoffined and stood upright in a vault, with their severed heads resting by their feet. The people of Dublin brought wreaths—and within a year, the moisture from the flowers had wrecked everything in that vault.

Not surprisingly, the tales of ghostly happenings pale in comparison to the gruesome reality of the crypt. But people exploring the macabre charnel house have heard strange and disembodied voices whispering around them, and some have felt ice-cold fingers run down their necks as they stoop to examine the permanent residents of this subterranean world of silent shadows.

KILLUA CASTLE
Killua, Westmeath

Killua Castle is a magnificent, romantic ruin that was once the seat of the Chapman family. Originally hailing from Leicestershire, England they obtained vast swathes of land in Ireland in the 16th century, thanks largely to the patronage of their famous cousin, Sir Walter Raleigh. However, it was a later family member, Benjamin, who, having fought as a captain in Cromwell's army, was awarded the confiscated lands of the Knights Hospitallers of St. John at Killua. The present structure of Killua Castle was built around 1780, although the conversion that created the rambling Gothic fantasy, the ruin of which greets the visitor today, was carried out in 1830. The last of the family line to be associated with the castle was Thomas Chapman, born in 1848, who married a girl from the Rochford family, by whom he had four children. The marriage was not a happy one, due largely to his wife's love of travel, and her long absences from home. Tiring of the situation, Thomas Chapman

finally abandoned his home, his wife, his family, and his name to live with his mistress, Sarah Dunner, in Wales, where he adopted the name Thomas Lawrence. The couple had seven children, one of whom, Thomas Edward Lawrence, would become the enigmatic and intriguing "Lawrence of Arabia."

A strange stillness hangs over this hollow castellated ruin today. The sheer number of dark empty window frames that greet your approach is enough to elicit cold shivers of an uncanny nature. The hollow rooms of the crumbling interior, where a time-worn stairway desperately clings to the ivy-clad walls, radiate a chilling feeling of melancholy, and you find yourself in constant fear of a chance encounter with the nebulous wraith of one of the castle's bygone residents.

No one is certain of the identity, or even the gender, of the white specter, whose shimmering shade has been seen wandering among the ruins at night. Suffice it to say that those who encounter "it" waste little time bothering to find out. Some people think that "it" is a "he," or to be precise, an 18th-century steward of the castle who, having turned to drink, was consumed with the terrors and tremors of dipsomania, and in despair drowned himself in a lake in the castle grounds.

However, other people voice the belief that the ghost is that of a daughter of the house who long ago met with a tragic accident, or was deserted by a feckless lover, or was subject to any one of the numerous sorrowful indignities that have, over the centuries, caused a glittering array of "white ladies" to slowly drift across the pages of folklore and legend the world over.

CASTLE LESLIE
Glaslough, Monaghan

Basking amid 1,000 acres of stunning scenery, the castle has been home to the exquisitely eccentric Leslie family for three hundred years. Today, the castle opens its doors to paying guests who find themselves transported in time to a bygone era. The Leslie family has, over the generations, played host to the likes of Dean Swift, W.B. Yeats, Sir John Betjeman, and Mick Jagger

The building that greets you today dates from 1878, and every one of its 14 bedrooms has a tale to tell. The Red Room is haunted by Norman Leslie, who was killed in action in 1914 and whose mother, Lady Marjorie, awoke here one night to find his ghost standing by the chest of drawers, surrounded by a "cloud of light." Norman's spirit was leafing through some letters and seemed to be seeking one in particular. Sitting up, she asked him "Why Norman—what are you doing here?" whereupon he turned to her, smiled and, faded away.

Time stands still at Castle Leslie, and its ambience is such that you find yourself wholeheartedly falling under the spell

of a family whose past eccentricities are a sheer joy to discover. Strange occurrences, such as mysterious gray figures twisting their way along atmospheric corridors and bells ringing of their own accord, seem positively mundane when pitted against the escapades of generations of Leslie's!

ABOVE: The Red Room in Castle Leslie, where the ghost of Norman Leslie occasionally makes an appearance.

and is generally accepted as little more than the oldest resident of this splendid old house.

SPRINGHILL
Near Moneymore, Londonderry

❈ ❈

Built in 1680 and once described as "the prettiest house in Ulster," Springhill stands as a proud testimony to successive generations of the Lenox-Conyngham family, whose home it was for nearly 300 years.

In 1816, George Lenox-Conyngham committed suicide, leaving his second wife, Olivia, to care for their children. Olivia was ever after haunted by remorse at her inability to prevent her husband's death, and her anguish appears to have followed her beyond the grave—for her ghost often appears at the house.

Olivia was seen in the early 20th century when the last generation of Lenox-Conyngham children to live at the property were sleeping one night—and their nursemaid awoke to find her gazing intently at the youngsters, as though checking the well-being of each one of them in turn. Today, Olivia's phantom still wanders the peaceful corridors of her old home. She exudes an aura of weary detachment

DOBBINS INN HOTEL
Carrickfergus, Antrim

❈ ❈

This hotel is the haunt of a ghostly lady whose name in life was Elizabeth, but who has long been known as "Maud." She lived in the 17th century, when the property was home to successive Mayors of Carrickfergus, one of whom, a member of the Dobbin family, was her husband.

Elizabeth is said to have become romantically involved with a soldier from nearby Carrickfergus Castle, whom tradition remembers simply as "buttoncap." At night, she would creep through a tunnel that linked the house and castle to meet with him. On discovering Elizabeth's infidelity, her husband murdered her as she entered the tunnel en route to an illicit liaison. Making his way to the castle, he then rushed upon the astonished "buttoncap" and beheaded him.

The ghost of Elizabeth Dobbin has wandered the building ever since, and staff have grown accustomed to her invisible shade gliding past them on her sorrowful quest to be reunited with her lover.

The WINDSWEPT LANDS *where* TERROR SAILED IN FROM THE SEA

On the lone bleak moor,   At the midnight hour,
    Beneath the Gallows Tree,
Hand in hand   The Murderers stand,
    By one, by two, or three!
And the Moon that night   With a gray, cold light
    Each baleful object tips;
One half of her form   Is seen through the storm,
    The other half's hid in Eclipse!
And the cold Wind howls,   And the Thunder growls,
    And the Lightning is broad and bright;
And altogether   It's very bad weather,
    And an unpleasant sort of a night!

FROM *THE HAND OF GLORY*
BY R.H. BARHAM

NORTH YORKSHIRE, LANCASHIRE, CUMBRIA, & NORTHUMBERLAND

From the urban spread of industrial Lancashire, through the magical and awesome scenery of the Lake District, the tranquil enchantment of Yorkshire to the wild and untamed Northumberland coast, the North of England comprises an area that revels in a stunning abundance of scenic delights. In the 8th century, Viking raiders brought terror to the ancient kingdom of Northumbria, on the northeast coast. As they moved inland and began to settle, they brought with them tales of dragons, ogres, trolls, and demon hounds, and supplanted these fearsome creatures into the dark places that Celtic legend had already imbued with an evil reputation. Their descendants would become the cattle stealers and ferocious warlords who ravaged and pillaged the Scottish border-lands throughout the Middle Ages. The memories of these unsettled times still linger in the gaunt ruins of the sturdy towers and castles that litter the region. The consequences of this rich and diverse brew of legend and warfare are apparent today in the wonderful variety of haunted places that the North has to offer.

KEY

1. Bagdale Hall
2. Goat Gap Inn
3. Newby Church
4. Treasurer's House
5. Trollers Gill
6. Pendle Hill
7. Smithills Hall
8. The Fairy Steps
9. Long Meg and her Daughters
10. Renwick
11. Dunstanburgh Castle
12. The Lord Crewe Arms
13. Winter's Gibbet

BAGDALE HALL
Whitby, North Yorkshire

Count Dracula's arrival in England one storm-racked August night must surely count as one of the most evocative and spine-tingling storm scenes ever written. By choosing Whitby as Dracula's landing place, Bram Stoker bestowed upon this pretty harbor town a sinister immortality, upon which it has capitalized ever since. Standing among the somber, gray-brown tombstones in the cliff-top churchyard of St. Mary's, and gaz-

ABOVE: Goat Gap Inn has a long tradition of being haunted by a ghostly drover named "George," who peaceably sits in a quiet corner of the bar.

ing down upon the red-tiled roofs, cobblestone streets, and sea-washed harbor walls, one is immediately struck by how little the vista has changed since Stoker found inspiration on its windswept heights. Nearby stands the stark ruin of Whitby Abbey. Following the abbey's dissolution by Henry VIII, its bells were removed, taken to the harbor, and loaded onto a ship bound for London. No sooner had the vessel set sail than it suddenly sank. The bells were never recovered, and it is said to be a good omen for lovers if they hear their ghostly peal sounding from beneath a storm-tossed sea on the night before Halloween.

Whitby's oldest building is thought to be Bagdale Hall, built in 1516 and now a hotel. A 17th-century owner named Browne Bushell, who was executed for piracy, is thought to haunt its ancient wooden staircase. Several housekeepers have sighted his phantom walking down the stairs toward them, with one even identifying a portrait of Browne Bushell as being the face of the specter she had just seen. Others, however, do not see him, but hear the tread of his footsteps as he passes by them unseen on the stairs. More recent phenomena have included cups of coffee being turned upside down by an unseen hand, the contents emptied onto the floor in front of witnesses; an ashtray slowly lifting from a table in the hotel's reception and dropping on the floor on the opposite side of the room; and disembodied children's voices sounding from empty rooms in the early hours of the morning.

GOAT GAP INN
Clapham, North Yorkshire

Situated on a lonely stretch of highway, this whitewashed stone inn, with its narrow corridors, low-beamed, dark

interior, and helicopter landing pad outside for those who wish to, literally, drop in for a pint, has a long tradition of being haunted. In one of the bedrooms, guests have watched in stunned silence as an unseen hand slowly turns on the hot faucet; in another room, residents have been disturbed by the sounds of childish voices singing a nursery rhyme.

The downstairs bar is the haunt of a cloth-capped, ghostly "George." George sits pensively in a corner by the window, his unblinking eyes gazing fixedly ahead, staring at nothing in particular. He is believed to be a former owner of the property from the days when the remote wayside inn was a tiny farmhouse. He bothers no one, and no one bothers him, as he occupies a favored position much as he may have done long ago in life, content to watch as the world passes by, although which world that is, no one knows for sure.

NEWBY CHURCH
Newby, North Yorkshire

In 1963, the Reverend Kenneth Lord was photographing the inside of his church. At the time, he saw nothing unusual through the viewfinder, and no one else was present in the building when he took the picture of the altar opposite. But when the photograph was developed, a tall, hooded figure was clearly visible standing in front of the deserted altar.

TREASURER'S HOUSE
York, North Yorkshire

Originally this was home to the treasurers of York Minster, who occupied the site from the 12th century until 1539, when Henry VIII's officers stripped the Minster of its assets during the Dissolution of the Monasteries. Although the last treasurer, William Clyffe, managed to cling to office for seven more years, he finally resigned his post in 1546 observing famously, "*Abrepto omni thesauro, desuit thesaurarii munus.*" ("There being no treasure left, there would seem to be no need for a treasurer.") The property then passed into private ownership and was largely rebuilt in the 17th century, although sections of the older building still survive in the cellar of the house.

It was in the cellar in 1953 that a young apprentice plumber, Harry Martindale, was working one day when he heard the sound of a distant trumpet. His puzzlement intensified when this was followed by a second blast, this time much closer and apparently behind him. Turning around, he was astonished when a horse's head suddenly emerged from the cellar wall. The rest of the horse's body, together with a ghostly rider dressed in the regalia of a Roman soldier, followed. The shock of the apparition sent the petrified apprentice tumbling from his ladder. Looking up, he saw other similarly attired figures following the horse and rider. Harry Martindale gazed in disbelief at the ragged detachment of around sixteen soldiers, all of whom were cut off at the knees. Their heads were downcast, giving them a gloomy aura of utter dejection, and their appearance was grubby and disheveled. They carried spears or swords, and wore plumed helmets and kilt-like skirts. They shuffled across to the opposite wall, where they melted slowly into the stone, and were gone. Racing from the cellar, Harry chanced upon the curator of the building, who took one look at his terrified face and said, "You've seen the Romans haven't you?"

It transpired that Harry Martindale was just one of a long line of people who had encountered the ghostly patrol in the cellar of the Treasurer's House. Intriguingly, later excavations unearthed a section of Roman road twelve or so inches beneath the floor of the cellar. The ghostly soldiers marching on this road would, as Harry had observed, give the appearance of being cut off at the knees.

ABOVE: It wasn't until he had his film developed that the Reverend Kenneth Lord noticed the ghostly figure standing to the right of the altar.

TROLLERS GILL
Appletreewick, North Yorkshire

The foaming brown waters that cascade through this dark ravine appear to be making a desperate attempt to flee the unfettered evil that seems to ooze from every pore of its sheer rock walls. Trees sprout from tiny crevices or cling desperately to the unrelenting slopes. Dark caves yawn, mysterious and forbidding, almost daring you to step beyond their jagged jaws and confront whatever malevolent forces might be lurking within.

Legend says that trolls live deep inside their icy depths. These dull-witted, hairy cannibals have stinking breath and huge noses that help them sniff out the blood of their human prey. At night they leave their cavernous vaults to patrol the gill, attacking lone wayfarers, exchanging human babies for their own offspring, and indulging in a lot of petty theft.

But worse still is the spectre of the "Barguest," a hideous, demon dog with long black hair and flaming eyes. His dreaded growl chills the blood of those who hear it, and the sound of his paws, padding across the cold wet rock, can reduce even the most intrepid wanderer to a nervous, shivering wreck. In the 19th

century, a young man, who sneered at such legends, is said to have entered the gill one night intent on capturing and enslaving the beast. His lifeless body was found the next morning, torn and bleeding on a rocky ledge. Massive claw marks were visible in deep gouges across his chest, and his face was hideously contorted, its frozen expression of abject terror a vivid testimony to his last desperate moments, spent gazing helplessly into the fiery eyes of the Barguest.

BELOW: The cellar of the Treasurer's House in York, where a detachment of Roman soldiers emerges from the walls and shuffles past astonished onlookers.

PENDLE HILL
Newchurch, Lancashire

❅❅❅❅❅❅❅❅❅❅❅❅❅❅❅❅❅❅❅❅❅❅❅

The brooding dome of Pendle Hill, its stark facade cracked by dark fissures and sinister ravines, dominates its surroundings. Beneath its lean slopes and within reach of its mighty shadow nestles the tiny village of Newchurch where, in the 17th century, a series of events occurred that have passed into folklore and legend.

For us today, in the enlightened world of mass communication, it is difficult to grasp the sheer terror that the mere threat of witchcraft could once evoke in such a small and isolated community. Yet the fact that for many years the villagers hereabouts lived in constant fear of the sinister sisterhood is aptly demonstrated by a curious oval stone that can be seen on the tower of the village's tiny church. It is known as the "Eye of God," and its purpose was to protect the villagers from the malign influences of the evil eye, one of the most feared weapons in a witch's arsenal of curses, spells, and potions.

In the early years of the 17th century, there lived on the slopes of Pendle Hill two feuding families headed by two old ladies named Demdike and Chattox. In March 1612, Demdike's granddaughter, Alizon Device, cursed an itinerant tailor who had refused to sell her some pins. Today, such behavior would be laughed off as nothing more than feuding, and the fact that the man was soon after rendered paralyzed, dismissed as mere coincidence. But the families already enjoyed a sinister reputation as witches and this, coupled with the fate of the tailor, spurred the authorities to action. Alizon Device was arrested and, under interrogation, confessed to witchcraft. She implicated Demdike and Chattox, who were brought before the powers that be, where they, too, admitted their guilt.

The three were sent to Lancaster Castle to await trial, and a subsequent investigation discovered seven more witches, including Alice Nutter, a gentlewoman from nearby Roughlee Hall. Demdike died in prison, but the others were tried for witchcraft, found guilty, and sentenced to death. The judge's comments that he had been moved by "the ruine of so many poore creatures at one time" were of little solace to the "Pendle Witches," who were hanged in Lancaster on August 20, 1612.

ABOVE: The church at Newchurch, where the saga of the so-called Pendle Witches unfolded.

BELOW: Mighty Pendle Hill, notorious for the feuding witches that lived upon its lower slopes in the 17th century.

SMITHILLS HALL
Bolton, Lancashire

❊ ❊ ❊ ❊ ❊ ❊ ❊ ❊ ❊ ❊ ❊ ❊ ❊ ❊ ❊ ❊ ❊ ❊ ❊ ❊

Situated on the outskirts of Bolton, Smithills Hall stands within the boundaries of its own country park and possesses a 14th-century Great Hall that is typical of a medieval fortified Lancashire manor house. Its low-beamed ceilings, uneven floors, and creaking staircases exude a timeless appeal that no amount of urban encroachment can subdue. The atmospheric rooms, resplendent with period furnishings, possess the true ambience of a bygone age, while the stone floor of one of the hall's ancient corridors presents even the most casual visitor with a tantalizing enigma to mull over.

Although a house has stood on this site since at least 1335, it was during the Marian persecutions of the 16th century that an event occurred that would, literally, leave a paranormal imprint upon the house's ancient fabric. As Mary Tudor strove to quash the Protestant faith and reintroduce Catholicism, several Anglican ministers bravely flouted her attempts. Among them was the Reverend George Marsh, who was brought to Smithills Hall to give account of his heresy to the hall's then owner, Robert Barton.

The interrogation is believed to have taken place in what is known as the "Green Room," and a contemporary description of thirty-one-year-old Barton as being "unwieldy, propped up in a well stuffed chair, one leg resting on a low stool, his whole frame bloated by indulgence and sensuality," is far from flattering. At one point in the long-winded proceedings, an exasperated George Marsh ran from the room, raced down the stairs, and stamped his foot hard upon the stone floor, crying as he did so, "If I am true to my faith, God shall leave his mark." Taken back to the room, the zealous vicar was ordered to stand trial for heresy. Found guilty, he was sentenced to death, and on April 24, 1555 was burned at the stake at Spittle-Boughton, outside Chester.

Robert's ghost is said to haunt the Green Room at Smithills Hall, but it is on the stone

floor at the foot of the staircase, where the frustrated martyr-to-be called upon God to leave his mark, that the most enduring and indelible reminder of that long-ago event can be seen. For there, preserved beneath a metal plate and clearly discernable on the stone, is the rough imprint of a man's foot, which is said to turn red and sticky every April 24.

THE FAIRY STEPS
Beetham, Cumbria

❊ ❊ ❊ ❊ ❊ ❊ ❊ ❊ ❊ ❊ ❊ ❊ ❊ ❊ ❊ ❊ ❊ ❊ ❊ ❊

A pleasant uphill stroll through the peaceful woods above the Lakeland village of Beetham leads to a tranquil little grotto, where a curious flight of tiny stone steps squeezes its way between the bulk of two sheer rock faces. Tradition has it that

RIGHT: Make a wish before descending the Fairy Steps, and reach the bottom without touching the sides, and your wish will be granted—but the demonic dog that haunts the rock might claim you first.

elfin craftsmen constructed this strange formation and, as a result, for as long as anyone can remember they have been known as the Fairy Steps.

It is said that if you make a wish as you begin the descent, and reach the bottom without having touched the sides, your wish will be granted. Sadly, only someone whose stature matches that of a fairy stands any chance of accomplishing the impossible feat, and those who attempt it would be better employed keeping a keen eye peeled for a more menacing inhabitant of this idyllic spot. He is a demon dog known as "the Cappel," and he prowls this rocky lair when the receding light of day has plunged the glade into nebulous shadow. To encounter his sinister form · is an omen of approaching bad luck. But to gaze into his fiery eyes, hear his low baleful growl, and smell his stinking breath is a portent of certain death.

BELOW: Legend tells that Long Meg, situated amid bleak and desolate terrain, was a 13th-century witch turned to stone by a medieval wizard.

LONG MEG AND HER DAUGHTERS
Glassonby, Cumbria

The remoteness of the location, coupled with the eerie bleakness of the surrounding hills lend this, one of England's largest stone circles, an aura of timeless mystery. Long Meg herself is an impressive megalith. She stands 18 feet high and arrogantly leans forward, dominating her fifty-nine daughters like a stern, stone matriarch.

The dry, dusty world of academia dates the stones from the period between the late Neolithic to early Bronze Age. The more inspired world of legend identifies them as a group of 13th-century witches, who were turned to stone by the renowned medieval wizard, Michael Scott. Here on this desolate, windswept plateau, the petrified sisterhood is condemned to stand, until the day dawns when someone succeeds in counting the same number of stones twice. The old magic radiates from this sullen group of rain-washed stones, and those who might consider damaging or mistreating either Meg or her daughters should heed the fate of the 18th-century farmer, whose attempts to remove the stones conjured up such a ferocious and terrible storm that he thought better of his actions and, wisely, desisted.

RENWICK
Cumbria

Renwick is a lonely and isolated village. It straddles a desolate stretch of wild moor, part of which is ominously named "Fiends Fell." Inside the village's pleasant, though otherwise uneventful, parish church, there is a faded typewritten script that details the intriguing story of how the villagers came by the sobriquet of "Renwick Bats."

It would seem that by 1733 the original church had fallen into disrepair, and it was decided that it should be rebuilt. But when the workmen had almost completed the

demolition of the old building, a hideous and ferocious creature suddenly flew at them from its foundations. They recognized it as a "cockatrice"—a mythical two-legged creature with the head of a cock, the body of a dragon, and the tail of a serpent—which, it was widely believed, in many countries across Europe and Asia, could kill its victims merely by looking at them. The workmen were, naturally, terrified and promptly downed tools and ran for their lives. All, that is, except John Tallantire, a brave and fearless man, who rushed at the dreadful creature and slew it with the branch of a rowan tree, a well-known protection against the evils of witchcraft.

Over years of retelling, the story has been toned down, and the more recent description of the creature as "a giant bat" is how the villagers' nickname came about. However, anyone who may be tempted to dismiss the tale as idle legend should take note of the number of people who, even within living memory, have witnessed a huge bat-like creature flying around the village in the fading light of day, or—worse still—have felt the evil chill of its dark shadow as it passes through the air above them.

DUNSTANBURGH CASTLE
Embleton, Northumberland

Sprawled across a windswept clifftop, against which thunderous waves incessantly pound,, the sinister ruins of Dunstanburgh Castle possess an uncanny aura that the proximity of a sea-sprayed golf course does little to dispel. Begun in 1316 by Thomas, Earl of Lancaster, and enlarged by John of Gaunt, the once proud fortress had, by the 16th century, fallen into decay, and was described in Henry VIII's reign as "a very ruinous house and of small strength."

Around this time, however, events occurred that have endowed the castle with a ghostly reputation. According to legend, Sir Guy the Seeker was a gallant knight who, while riding along the Northumberland coast one day, found himself caught in a dreadful storm. Desperate for shelter, he chanced upon the ruins of Dunstanburgh Castle and, leading his terrified horse up the perilous and twisting rocky path, took sanctuary from the tempest beneath the shattered turrets of its massive gatehouse. As the storm raged and the

BELOW: The sinister ruins of Dunstanburgh Castle, where a ghostly knight still seeks a "beauty bright."

ABOVE: Ghostly monks are just some of several specters that disturb the sleepy ambience of Blanchland village.

her. He thought for a moment and then, striding forward, took up the horn and blew it. Suddenly, the sleeping knights flashed into life and rushed at him, whereupon Sir Guy fainted clean away. As the room began to swirl, the figure in white came toward him, a look of contempt upon its twisted features—and as he slipped into unconsciousness, he heard its taunting voice, echoing round and round inside his head: "Now shame on the coward who sounded a horn, and the knight who sheathed a sword."

When Sir Guy regained consciousness, he was lying beneath the ruins of the gatehouse. From that day forth, he was determined to find the sleeping maiden again. It became an obsession as he rummaged around every corner of the moldering ruin. But he never again found the room in which she lay, and he died a broken, lonely old man. On windswept, stormy days, as the waves thunder against the castle rock, and the winds howl through the ruins, his ghost is said to wander the stark passages and winding stone staircases, still seeking the "beauty bright" amid the savage remnants of this imposing edifice.

THE LORD CREWE ARMS
Blanchland, Northumberland

The sleepy ambience of Blanchland village evokes a poignant nostalgia for a slower, more genteel age. Its 18th-century stone cottages are laid out along the foundations of Blanchland Abbey, to whose plan the village remains true.

The abbey was founded in 1165 by the Premonstratension order, whose distinctive white habits gave the village its name "Blancalande," meaning "white land." Its isolated location meant that daily life was a constant struggle, the problems being compounded by the danger of savage raids from the "border reivers." One day, a party of these feared and ferocious outlaws are said to have set out for the abbey intent on murder, pillage, and plunder. The monks received word of their approach and began making preparations. But suddenly, a dense fog descended, causing the raiding party to become disoriented. Convinced that the miraculous mist was nothing short of divine intervention, the monks gave thanks by letting out a joyous peal of the abbey bells. It was an ill-conceived act of piety. Their would-be attackers simply followed the sound, and concluded their bloody business by massacring all the monks. On certain days of the year, the bells of the village church are said to ring of their own accord as the misty wraiths of the murdered monks are seen around the churchyard.

wind howled through the crevices of the castle walls, there appeared a hideous figure dressed in white that urged him to follow it to where he would be rewarded by a "beauty bright."

The fearless knight followed the figure up a narrow winding staircase and into a room where lay a hundred sleeping knights and their horses. At the center of the chamber, in a sparkling crystal casket, there slept the most beautiful maiden Sir Guy had ever seen. On either side of her were two serpents, one holding a sword, the other a horn. The specter told Sir Guy that he could awaken the lady, but that he must choose whether to use the sword or the horn. Only the correct choice would rouse

"NOW SHAME ON THE COWARD WHO SOUNDED A HORN, AND THE KNIGHT WHO SHEATHED A SWORD."

THE SPECTER TO SIR GUY THE SEEKER AT DUNSTANBURGH

Next door to the church is what must surely count as one of England's most characterful hotels, The Lord Crewe Arms. It was formerly the abbot's guesthouse, and its ancient stone walls, barrel-vaulted crypt bar, low-beamed ceilings, and massive fireplaces, one of which contains a cleverly concealed "priest's hide," positively crackle with atmosphere.

A building of such impressive antiquity inevitably harbors several ghosts behind its inviting facade. In the late 1990s, an American guest who was sleeping in the Radcliffe Room awoke in the early hours one morning to find a monk, dressed in a white habit, kneeling at the end of the four-poster bed. Unperturbed by the apparition, she reached down and touched him, finding him to be "quite solid." But no sooner had she done so than he became hazy and melted into thin air.

Best-known of all the hotel's ghosts, however, is that of Dorothy Forster, who was the sister of Tom Forster, the unwilling commander of the Jacobite forces during the 1715 uprising. Poor Tom had no qualifications and even fewer natural instincts for such an important position, and when confronted by his adversaries at Preston, he surrendered without attempting to fight. Taken to London and held in Newgate Prison, Tom awaited his inevitable fate. But Dorothy engineered his escape just three days before he was due to stand trial. He was brought to The Lord Crewe Arms and hidden in the priest's hide behind the fireplace until it was deemed safe to smuggle him out of the country to France.

Sadly, brother and sister never saw each other again, for Tom Forster died in France. Dorothy stayed behind at The Lord Crewe Arms and has remained there ever since. Many is the night that guests sleeping in the Bamburgh Room have been woken by her sad specter imploring them to relay the message to her brother in France that all is now well, and he can safely return to England.

WINTER'S GIBBET
Elsdon, Northumberland

Elsdon Moor is a wild and windswept wilderness. Traversing its bleak expanse of green turf and purple heather, with a leaden sky skulking overhead, can be a strange and unnerving experience. The feeling of tense unease increases sharply when you stumble upon the replica of Winter's Gibbet, silhouetted against the drifting clouds. It stands where the body of William Winter, executed for the murder of Margaret Crozier in 1791, was hung in chains and left to rot as a dire warning to others who might contemplate similar crimes. Today, a

chain, from which dangles the image of a human head, hangs from the gibbet's beam, clanking eerily with the breeze.

The area around the gibbet is the reputed haunt of the "Brown Man of the Moor," a red-haired dwarf with ferocious countenance and "eyes glowing like those of a bull." It is his solemn duty to punish those who harm any of the creatures who roam the wild landscape. An 18th-century hunter who disregarded the Brown Man's warning to desist from his sport was suddenly taken ill and died a few days later. And even today, several people traipsing home in fading light have caught fleeting glimpses of a red-headed specter who appears to be keeping a wary eye on them.

BELOW: A feeling of unease emanates from the stark replica of Winter's Gibbet, where the Brown Man of the Moor brings death to all who harm his subjects, the wild animals.

BLOODIED LAND of KINGS and CASTLES

My hopes are with the Dead; anon
My place with them will be,
And I with them shall travel on
Through all Futurity;
Yet leaving here a name, I trust,
That will not perish in the dust.

FROM *THE SCHOLAR*
BY ROBERT SOUTHEY

SCOTLAND

Scotland was for centuries a divided nation, and its history is spattered with the blood of countless conflicts, many of them fought between the Highlanders and the Lowlanders. Only very occasionally did the two bury their differences to unite against a common enemy, as successive English kings strove to invade and conquer. They fought with an indomitable spirit, as the likes of William Wallace and Robert the Bruce inspired their kinsmen to stand firm against their English adversaries.

Today, vestiges of this stormy past are to be found all over Scotland. Ruined forts, silent reminders of old frontier wars, stud the landscape on both sides of the border with England. Impressive stone castles can be found all over the country, from the gentle farmlands of the Central Lowlands to the wild empty lands of Europe's last great wilderness in the country's northwest. Scotland's ghosts are perpetual reminders of the conflicts that have raged throughout the land. Kings, queens, Highlanders, and Lowlanders inhabit the ethereal domain where old feuds and differences have never died, and ancient conflicts are fought time and again before astonished witnesses.

KEY
1. Hermitage Castle
2. Tibbie Shiel's Inn
3. Linlithgow Palace
4. Rosslyn Chapel
5. Mary King's Close
6. Blackness Castle
7. Culcreach Castle
8. The Pass of Killiecrankie
9. Glamis Castle
10. Skibo Castle
11. Eilean Donan Castle
12. Sandwood Bay

HERMITAGE CASTLE
Newcastleton, Borders
❊ ❊

Hermitage Castle is a squat, gaunt and forbidding fortress that broods in desolate isolation, amid some of the eeriest countryside imaginable. The gentle warmth of a summer's

PREVIOUS PAGES: A dark secret is said to be hidden within a secret room behind the fairytale facade of Glamis Castle, Scotland's most haunted abode.

morning rarely penetrates its sullen bulk. Creepy corridors and cold, stone staircases snake their way between the moss-covered walls of its melancholic interior, while a menacing aura of genuine evil seems to emanate from its very fabric.

The castle was built around 1300 on the disputed borderlands between England and Scotland. Over the next four hundred years it would regularly change hands between the two countries, and the frequent conflicts led to its being dubbed the "guardhouse to the bloodiest valley in Britain." In 1342, Sir Alexander Ramsey found himself imprisoned at Hermitage in "a frightful pit or dungeon, apparently airless and devoid of sanitation." Here he was starved to death, and

ABOVE: Gaunt and forbidding Hermitage Castle is haunted by the terrifying figure of "Bad" Lord de Soulis.

his sad, hungry ghost has wandered through the castle and grounds ever since.

One of the most infamous early owners was "Bad" Lord de Soulis, a renowned practitioner of the black arts who, it was rumored, used the dungeons of the castle to hold captive the children of the neighborhood, whom he had kidnapped for use in his sinister rituals. The local residents petitioned King Robert I, begging him to relieve them of the wicked lord. "Boil him if you must," replied the king, "but let me hear no more of him." Taking their monarch's words literally, the furious locals stormed the castle, captured de Soulis, wrapped him in

lead, and threw him into a boiling cauldron. His malevolent specter has walked the grounds and corridors ever since, his nebulous meanderings often accompanied by the poignant sounds of children's screams, echoing from somewhere deep beneath the castle.

There is something indefinable about the atmosphere of Hermitage Castle, as though whatever malevolent forces are harbored within this impregnable and thoroughly demonic fortress resent your presence. The frequent reports of ghostly figures seen flitting about the upper stories in the dead of night certainly elicit cold shivers, and you find yourself constantly looking over your shoulder, ever wary of who, or even what, might be lurking around the next corner, or waiting just a few rooms along.

TIBBIE SHIEL'S INN
St. Mary's Loch, Borders

❈❈❈❈❈❈❈❈❈❈❈❈❈❈❈❈❈❈❈❈❈

In 1823, following the death of her husband, Isabelle Shiel was left destitute and penniless. But with commendable determination, this formidable lady—who preferred to be known as "Tibbie"—opened a beer house on the picturesque shores of St. Mary's Loch, and soon succeeded in reversing her fortunes. By the time of her death, at the ripe old age of 96, such was her fame that the inn could count the likes of Sir Walter Scott, Thomas Carlyle, and Robert Louis Stevenson as past customers. Her mortal remains were laid to rest in nearby Ettrick Kirkyard, but her guiding spirit remained at the inn to ensure that the business she had founded survived, and that it continued to operate with the smooth efficiency her clients had come to expect.

Even today, many guests who come to enjoy the idyllic setting of the inn have sometimes encountered her wraith silently flitting across their bedrooms in the early hours of the morning. Patrons of the downstairs bar have been startled by the eerie touch of an invisible, cold, and clammy hand upon their shoulders, while a group of hikers, who were hogging the fire one cold winter's day in 1999, were astonished when the poker was suddenly lifted from the fire by an invisible hand and waved at them in menacing rebuke.

LINLITHGOW PALACE
Linlithgow, West Lothian

❈❈❈❈❈❈❈❈❈❈❈❈❈❈❈❈❈❈❈❈❈

From the moment you pass into the gloomy, hollow shell of Linlithgow Palace and gaze upon its towering, red stone walls, a sense of awestruck wonderment seizes your imagination. The palace was built in the early part of the 15th century by King James I of Scotland, and was subsequently enlarged by successive monarchs. Mary, Queen of Scots was born here in 1542, and it was last used as a Royal palace by King Charles I in 1633. In 1746 General Hawley retreated here, following his defeat by Jacobite forces at Falkirk. His rain-drenched soldiers lit a fire by which to dry themselves and accidentally set the palace ablaze. It was never rebuilt, and its evocative ruins now stand as proud testimony to its eventful past, while several ghosts wander its twisting corridors, winding stairways, and dark, vaulted rooms. Inevitably, Mary, Queen of Scots has been seen on more than one occasion, and seems to favor the region of the chapel. But the most persistent spectral visitor is the white-clad wraith of a mysterious woman whose approach is announced by a distinct drop in temperature, and whose passage is marked by a delicate perfume, the delightful smell of which has been commented on by more than one visitor. In 1999, a steward who lives nearby was visited one night by a man who insisted that someone was locked inside the palace. The steward shook her head, saying that it was impossible. But the man was convinced that he had seen a woman in a white dress walking around inside the building. The two of them went back to the palace, unlocked the door, and searched the whole interior, finding no one. "Don't worry," the steward told him, "you've seen the ghost; I see her all the time."

ROSSLYN CHAPEL
Roslin, Midlothian

❈❈❈❈❈❈❈❈❈❈❈❈❈❈❈❈

Menacing grotesques scowl a fiendish welcome as you approach the ornate, though decaying, stone doorway of this mysterious chapel, which is steeped in myth and legend. It was founded by Sir William St Clair, Prince of Orkney in 1446, and its interior must surely rate as one of the most exquisite of any chapel in Britain. The barrel-vaulted roof is richly adorned with delicate carvings of daisies, lilies, roses, and stars. Angelic figures engaged in all manner of heavenly activity are molded around the walls, but so, too, are stone demons, saints, martyrs, lions, and even pagan green men. Elsewhere, a ferocious dragon coils around intricately carved column that is known as the "Apprentice" or "Prentice Pillar." The story behind the creation of this famous pillar is both fascinating and tragic.

The master mason was requested by St. Clair to carve this particular pillar in the style of a specific one he had seen in Rome. Unwilling to commence work without first viewing the original, the master set off for Rome to prepare for the task. While he was away, his apprentice dreamed that it was he who had finished the column, and with the details still fresh in his mind, set to work on carving the pillar himself. When the master returned, he is said to have been so envious at the

superior skill demonstrated by his pupil that he flew into a rage and struck the unfortunate boy across the head with a mallet, killing him instantly. The master was hanged for his crime, and the boy's ghost has haunted the chapel ever since. He is seen standing by the column, gazing at it with a look of mournful longing etched across his face. Some visitors have also heard the sound of weeping, apparently emanating from within the column itself. Elsewhere in the chapel, there is still a poignant reminder of the long-ago tragedy. Gazing down from the walls to the right and left of the organ loft are the carved images of the unfortunate apprentice (complete with head wound), his grieving mother, and the murderous master.

MARY KING'S CLOSE
Edinburgh

❋❋❋❋❋❋❋❋❋❋❋❋❋❋❋❋❋❋❋❋❋❋❋

Standing in the dark, narrow streets and closes (or passages) that slope steeply between the tall gaunt buildings lining the ridge known as the Royal Mile, in Edinburgh, you find yourself lost in an almost ethereal world of silent shadow. In the Middle Ages, this was one of the most densely populated and disease-ridden quarters in Europe, and you entered these sinister labyrinths at your peril. Confined by the city wall, Edinburgh expanded upward, its stark tenements rising nine, ten, even eleven, stories high, casting the walkways between

ABOVE: The Rosslyn Chapel, one of the most mystical and elaborate foundations in the whole of Britain.

OPPOSITE: Since her execution in 1587, Mary, Queen of Scots has become one of Britain's most-seen ghosts.

them into permanent darkness. Even today, a journey through these murky chasms is not for the faint of heart, and the tales of ghosts and sinister happenings, of which there are plenty, can elicit cold shivers, even on the brightest summer's day.

Buried beneath the 18th-century buildings of the city chambers there exists a hidden place—Mary King's Close—that is historically more horrifying, and supernaturally more terrifying, than any other. Plague was a frequent visitor to the squalid and rat-infested tenements of Edinburgh. But one of the worst visitations came in 1645, and the residents of Mary King's and neighboring closes were decimated by it. The city fathers, in an ill-conceived and barbaric attempt to contain the contagion, walled these neighborhoods off, leaving the residents to die in what must have been unimaginable horror.

Once the pestilence had abated, the stench from the corpses became unbearable, so the authorities sent two butchers to clear away the detritus of the deceased. The men simply hacked the rotting cadavers to pieces, loaded them onto a cart, and wheeled them away. Such was the shortage of accommodation, that soon new residents came to live in Mary King's Close, and by 1685 it had become common knowledge that spirits from the plague year were still there. Thomas Coltheart, a lawyer, and his wife were beset in their new home by numerous apparitions. The disembodied head of an old man, with a wispy, gray beard and terrible eyes, was seen floating around their rooms. It was sometimes accompanied by a severed arm, which seemed intent on shaking Thomas Coltheart's hand. A ghostly child appeared hovering in midair, as well as a menagerie of deformed phantom animals.

The upper stories of the close were demolished in 1750, and the Royal Exchange was constructed on the site. The city merchants, however, preferred to do business in the streets, and so the new building became the City Chambers, beneath which the rooms and passage of Mary King's Close survived.

Today, it is a secret place that can be visited only on pre-booked tours. It is also reputed to be the most haunted part of Edinburgh. A tall lady, dressed in a long black gown, is but one of the many ghosts that frequent this underground world. Several visitors have caught fleeting glimpses of a short, elderly man who bears a troubled expression. But perhaps the most poignant of its earthbound spirits is that of a little girl, whose lank hair hangs over a pale face that is covered in weeping sores. She was discovered by a Japanese medium, brought here by a television company, who was told nothing of the close's history prior to her visit. Stepping into one of the rooms, the medium was overwhelmed by a disturbingly depressive aura. As she turned to leave, someone tugged on her trouser leg. Going back into the room, she found a disheveled young girl weeping in the corner, who told her that she had died of "the sickness" in 1645. The distraught child revealed that she had lost her doll and felt very lonely and unhappy as a result. Moved by her plight, the television crew bought her a doll and left it in the room. Ever since, visitors have brought gifts for the ghost, and a collection of toys, dolls, books, and coins is now piled in the corner of the room.

BLACKNESS CASTLE
Blackness, Stirlingshire
❄ ❄

Your worst nightmares could not conjure up a place as demonic as the aptly named Blackness Castle. It squats

BELOW: The grim bulk of the aptly named Blackness Castle squats on its menacing, rocky throne and possesses a truly evil aura.

menacingly atop a knoll of jagged black rock, its shoreline lapped by the gray waters of the Firth of Forth. From the moment you set foot on the rickety pathway of its vaulted gatehouse, you are confronted by a sparse interior, where foreboding oozes from its every pore. As you wander between its forbidding towers, you don't so much walk as stumble across the uneven cobblestones, or scramble across chunks of black, serrated rock to reach rooms and staircases where you sense that numerous unspeakable deeds have been perpetrated.

Built in the 14th century, and massively strengthened in the 16th century when it became an artillery fortress, it has also been a Royal castle, an armaments depot, and a state prison. The central tower is known as the "Prison Tower" and, as you climb its winding, stone staircase, a feeling of oppressive coldness hangs heavy in the air. It was here that a dramatic manifestation occurred in the late 1990s, when a lady who had brought her two young sons on a visit was startled by the appearance of a knight in armor whom, she claimed, angrily chased her from the tower. A group of ghost enthusiasts, who persuaded the custodian to allow them to stay overnight one Halloween, were disturbed by the constant noise of furniture being scraped and banged across the stone floor of the room beneath them. Although one of their number investigated the disturbance, he found nothing out of place, but the moment he returned to his companions, the noises began again.

CULCREUCH CASTLE
Fintry, Stirlingshire

❧❧❧❧❧❧❧❧❧❧❧❧❧❧❧❧❧❧❧❧❧❧❧

In 1296, Maurice Gailbraith, son of a Gailbraith chief, began the construction of Kilcreuch Castle, and laid the foundations of the home of the Clan Gailbraith. They were a warlike family who burned, looted, murdered, pillaged, and raped their way through three hundred years of bloody history. In short, they were a thoroughly bad lot, and few tears were shed when in 1630, Robert, the debt-ridden seventeenth Gailbraith Chief, surrendered the castle to his creditors and fled to Ireland.

With the passing years, Kilcreuch became Culcreuch. The

ABOVE: The antique Chinese wallpaper of Culcreuch Castle's Chinese Bird Room is justly famous, and guests can expect to be lulled to sleep by the soothing strings of a ghostly harp.

castle passed through several ownerships and is now a magnificent hotel, set amid 1,600 spectacular acres reached via a picturesque drive that meanders its way along the tree-lined banks of a serene lake. The castle boasts three ghosts. First, there is a severed boar's head lain upon a silver salver, which has been seen flying around the battlements and then plummeting toward the ground, where it always vanishes just before impact. Second, there is the "moving, cold gray mass of turbulence, the height and size of a human," which several guests have felt brushing by in the bedrooms and corridors.

The best-attested of the phantoms haunts the world-famous Chinese Bird Room, where the handpainted wallpaper, depicting colorful birds and exotic palms, is the only example of genuine antique Chinese wallpaper in Scotland. The origins of the haunting date back to 1582, when Robert Gailbraith was entertaining a member of the neighboring Buchanan Clan and his mistress to a banquet at the castle. Following a heated exchange between the two men, Robert leapt to his feet and stabbed his guest who, legend says, was taken to what is now the Chinese Bird Room, where his distraught mistress tended his wounds. In the early hours of the morning, he expired in her arms. Taking up her harp, she began to pick at its strings to soothe her grief, and her ghost has done so ever since. Many guests staying in the room have found themselves lulled into a peaceful sleep by the soothing tones of her ghostly harp.

THE PASS OF KILLIECRANKIE
Pitlochry, Perthshire

❊❊❊❊❊❊❊❊❊❊❊❊❊❊❊❊❊❊❊❊❊❊

Killiecrankie, a name derived from Gaelic and meaning "wood of aspens," is a tranquil oasis, set amid dramatic and spectacular scenery. The distant views of moody, gray mountains, the foaming waters of the River Garry tumbling between steeply wooded cliffs, and the picturesque pathways that twist their way through the dense undergrowth all combine to lend the gorge a soothing aura of peaceful detachment. But scattered around its tree-lined tracks are numerous reminders of a long-ago sunset, when the sudden sound of gunfire shattered the stillness, and a bloody battle exploded across the sylvan slopes of the ravine.

The Battle of Killiecrankie took place on July 27, 1689. It was fought between 3,400 government troops, loyal to William of Orange and led by General Mackay, and 2,500 Jacobite Highlanders, supporters of the deposed king, James VII of Scotland (James II of England), commanded by Viscount John Graham of Claverhouse, known as "Bonnie Dundee."

As the opposing armies faced each other amid the woodlands of Killiecrankie, the smaller Jacobite force claimed the higher ground and waited for the sun to move behind them, before Dundee gave the order to charge. Dazzled by the sun, the government troops watched helplessly as a screaming avalanche of tartan terror swept down the slopes of the gorge toward them. As the Royalist soldiers scattered, the ferocious Highlanders threw down their muskets and continued the fray with the flash of cold steel. A government soldier

LEFT: The tranquil Pass of Killiecrankie, where reminders of a bloody conflict are scattered across the pathways, and a ghostly red glow is sometimes seen on the slopes.

OPPOSITE: Ghosts galore are known to walk the corridors and passageways of Glamis Castle where, according to Shakespeare, Macbeth slew King Duncan.

named Donald Macbear took one look at the advancing hoard and, pursued by a gaggle of deadly Highlanders, ran for his life. Arriving at the rocky shore of the River Garry, he escaped by jumping 18 feet to its opposite bank, leaving his pursuers gazing in astonished fury across the gap, which is still known "'Soldier's Leap" in commemoration of the amazing feat. By the time the sun sank over the battlefield, the Jacobite troops had inflicted a crushing defeat upon the government forces. But their victory was a hollow one, for Bonnie Dundee suffered a fatal wound as he waved his Highland warriors on to victory. The Jacobite force never really recovered from his death, and their army was later forced to disband after failing to capture Dunkeld.

In the Pass of Killiecrankie, a dull, red glow has been known to bathe the area in its ruddy hue on the anniversary of the battle. Some people have been startled by the sudden appearance of ghostly troops marching through the ravine in the fading light. Others have heard the distinct volley of invisible muskets firing in the air. One woman looked up from a picnic she was enjoying to see the phantom forms of several dead soldiers lying on the ground nearby!

GLAMIS CASTLE
Forfar, Angus

❊❊❊❊❊❊❊❊❊❊❊❊❊❊❊❊❊❊❊❊❊❊

Set against the stunning backdrop of the Grampian Mountains, the soaring towers and lofty battlements of Glamis Castle are both enchanting and mysterious. It is the seat of the Earl of Strathmore and Kinghorne and dates back to the 15th century, although much of what survives today is of a later date. Shakespeare made Macbeth "Thane of Glamis," and set the murder of King Duncan within the castle's gloomy walls, although the slaying actually took place near Elgin. Much of the castle was rebuilt in the 17th century, when it acquired its French chateau look. In the early part of the 20th century, it was the childhood home of Lady Elizabeth Bowes-Lyon, who would later become the Queen Mother.

At least six ghosts are known to wander its rooms and corridors. One of them haunts the atmospheric crypt, reached via a connecting door from the splendid Dining Room, which, in an instant, transports visitors from the stately opulence of the Victorian era to the more austere days of the Middle Ages. Behind one of the thick, stone walls exists a secret chamber, around which are woven many legends. It was here that one of the Lords of Glamis, "Earl Beardie" as he was known, was playing cards with the "Tiger" Earl of Crawford and was reluctant to give up the game, even though the Sabbath was rapidly approaching. No sooner had the clock chimed midnight, than the devil appeared and asked to join the game. The rash Earl Beardie promptly gambled away his soul, and died soon after. For many years, the sounds of

> **"I BEGAN To CoNSIDER MYSELF AS TOO FAR FROM THE LIVING AND SoMEWHAT TOO NEAR THE DEAD."**
>
> WALTER SCOTT, COMMENTING ON HIS VISIT TO GLAMIS CASTLE

cursing and swearing were heard echoing from the room at night and, in an attempt to quell the disturbances, the chamber was bricked up. But the foul-mouthed phantom could not be confined, and his fearsome specter is still said to roam the castle in the dead of night. There are several reports of guests waking to find him leaning over their beds, gazing at them with evil intent.

The castle's peaceful little chapel is the haunt of the "Gray Lady," thought to be the ghost of Janet Douglas, wife of John, the sixth Lord Glamis. King James V hated the Douglas Clan, on account of the fact that he had been completely dominated by his Douglas stepfather and manipulated by other members of the family. Following the death of her husband, Janet married Archibald Campbell of Skipness and brought him to live at Glamis. But James had been waging a ruthless vendetta against the Douglas Clan and, in what can only be described as an act of petulant spite, he turned his attentions to the popular and beautiful Lady Campbell and had her arrested on a trumped-up charge of witchcraft. On July 17, 1537, she was led from Edinburgh Castle and burned at the stake on Castlehill. Her ghost has been seen many times in the chapel, kneeling in silent prayer, a shimmering, translucent figure who exudes an aura of peaceful tranquillity and melts into nothingness after a few short moments.

Glamis Castle has many secrets, and its walls must have borne silent witness to thousands of tragic and sinister events. Wandering its rooms, corridors, and staircases, you can almost sense the eyes of past occupants watching your progress, and it is easy to sympathize with the sentiments expressed by Sir Walter Scott when he visited: "I began to consider myself as too far from the living and somewhat too near the dead."

SKIBO CASTLE
Dornoch, Sutherland

Set amid 7,500 acres of stunning scenery, ancient Skibo Castle was once home to successive bishops of Caithness, until the Church relinquished ownership to the Gray Clan in 1565. Many decades later, a local girl is said to have disappeared after setting off to visit the castle. It was always supposed that she had been murdered by the Castle's keeper and her body hidden within its grounds. Soon afterward, there were rumors of a ghostly "white lady" who flitted through the building at night, her nocturnal jaunts always accompanied by sorrowful moans and terrified screams. During later renovations, a woman's skeleton was found hidden behind one of the castle walls and, when the grisly remains received a formal burial, the haunting ceased, but only for a time.

In 1898, the American millionaire Andrew Carnegie acquired the ruined estate and set about a lavish rebuilding program, the result of which was the spectacular castle that greets visitors today. Few could argue with his description of it as "heaven on earth," despite the presence of the fabled "white lady," who has returned several times to explore its corridors and richly adorned rooms. Carnegie's grandson, Rosewell Miller III, encountered the female phantom one night as she drifted silently along a third floor corridor and turned into one of the many bedrooms. Bemused by her strange appearance, Rosewell followed her into the room, but could find no trace of the mysterious apparition.

The building today houses the Carnegie Club, where visitors can experience the true ambience of a bygone era by imagining themselves the house guests at a great sporting estate of the Edwardian period. Such is its exclusivity, that guests are allowed to stay only once in their lifetime, after which they must be proposed and accepted for membership if they wish to enjoy a return visit. On December 22, 2000, Skibo Castle was catapulted into the international spotlight, when pop diva Madonna and film director Guy Ritchie chose it as the stunning highland venue for what was dubbed "the showbiz wedding of the decade." Whether any of the assembled throng of the world's glitterati encountered Skibo's ghostly "white lady" is yet to be revealed!

BELOW: Skibo Castle is a romantic place to hold a wedding, but guests should watch out for ghosts.

EILEAN DONAN CASTLE
Kyle of Lochalsh, Highlands

❊❊❊❊❊❊❊❊❊❊❊❊❊❊❊❊❊❊❊❊❊

Alexander II built one of Scotland's most picturesque strongholds, Eilean Donan Castle, in 1220. It stands on an island at the meeting point of Lochs Duich, Alsh, and Long, its image rippling in the silent waters, reflecting past eras of grandeur and mystery. Robert the Bruce sheltered here in 1306—and Randolph, Earl of Moray, had fifty men executed here in 1331 and then displayed their heads on spikes around the castle walls. During the 1719 Jacobite uprising, the sympathetic William MacKenzie, fifth Earl of Seaforth, garrisoned the castle with Spanish troops. Three English frigates, led by the warship *Worcester*, unleashed a bombardment of artillery against the defenders, battered them into submission, and left the castle little more than a moldering ruin. It was rebuilt in 1932 by the MacRae family, and is now a Clan war memorial and museum. It is haunted by one of the Spanish soldiers who died in the unrelenting bombardment, and who is said to wander the castle, carrying his head under his arm.

SANDWOOD BAY
Kinlochbervie, Highlands

❊❊❊❊❊❊❊❊❊❊❊❊❊❊❊❊❊❊❊❊❊

Sandwood Bay sits in utter isolation on the very tip of northwest Scotland. It is, perhaps, one of Britain's most remote spots. No roads lead to it, and those who make the effort to walk the rough track across peat bogs and empty moorland

ABOVE: Eilean Donan Castle is haunted by a phantom that carries its own grisly head.

to reach its pale, pink sands are rewarded with a vista of such untamed splendor that they can easily imagine they have reached the edge of the physical world. But a strange, uncanny feeling of indefinable unease often taints the beauty. Perhaps it is the number of ships wrecked off Cape Wrath, whose shattered remnants and drowned crews were carried by the currents into Sandwood Bay, that have left a psychic imprint on the surrounds. Whatever the cause, visitors have been complaining of the creepy aura for centuries, and some who venture to this wild cove have caught fleeting glimpses of a ghostly sailor striding across the sand. Others have been treated to a full-fledged manifestation in which the salty old sea dog looks so lifelike that they have attempted to engage him in conversation.

There have been reports of the strange apparition since the early years of the 20th century. He has been seen by walkers, crofters, and visitors and was, on one famous occasion, even chased by a gamekeeper who mistook him for a poacher. He is always described as a stocky, bearded figure wearing a sailor's cap, black boots, and reefer jacket resplendent with gleaming brass buttons. No matter how far he walks across the beach, he never leaves behind any footprints. Whoever he was, and whatever the reason behind his daytime visits to this remote and beautiful inlet, he has left in his wake numerous bemused witnesses, and his fame is such that several visitors now make the exhaustive hike to Sandwood Bay for no other reason than the possibility of a chance encounter with its ghostly sailor.

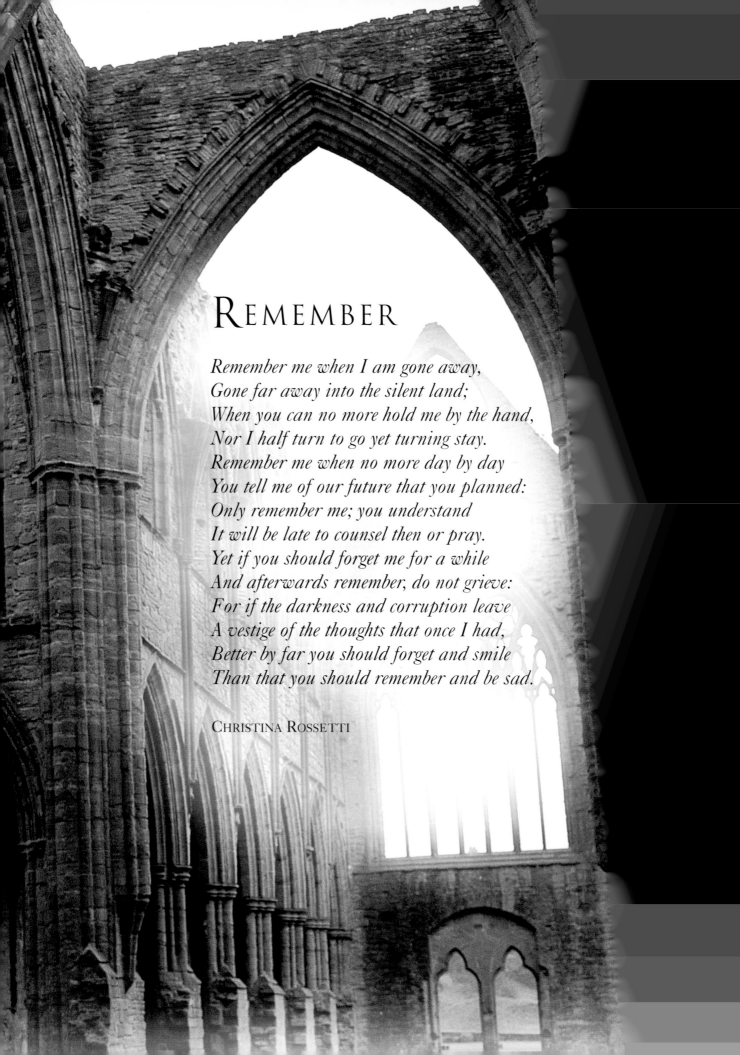

REMEMBER

Remember me when I am gone away,
Gone far away into the silent land;
When you can no more hold me by the hand,
Nor I half turn to go yet turning stay.
Remember me when no more day by day
You tell me of our future that you planned:
Only remember me; you understand
It will be late to counsel then or pray.
Yet if you should forget me for a while
And afterwards remember, do not grieve:
For if the darkness and corruption leave
A vestige of the thoughts that once I had,
Better by far you should forget and smile
Than that you should remember and be sad.

CHRISTINA ROSSETTI

RECOMMENDED READING

Abbott, Geoffrey *Ghosts of the Tower of London*, Heinemann, 1980

Adams, Norman *Haunted Scotland*, Mainstream, 1998

Alexander, Marc *Phantom Britain*, Muller, 1975

Brooks, J. A. *Ghosts and Witches of the Cotswolds* Jarrold, 1981

Brooks, J. A. *Ghosts and Legends of the Lake District*, Jarrold, 1988

Byrne, Thomas *Tales From The Past*, Ironmarket, 1977

Clarke, David *Ghosts and Legends of the Peak District*, Jarrold, 1991

Coventry, Martin *Haunted Places of Scotland*, Goblinshead, 1999

Coxe, Anthony D. Hippisley *Haunted Britain*, Pan, 1975

Crowe, Catharine *The Night Side of Nature*, Wordsworth Editions, 2000

Curran, Bob *Banshees, Beasts and Brides From the Sea* Appletree Press, 1996

Dunne, John J. *Irish Ghosts* Appletree Press, 1977

Folklore, Myths and Legends of Britain, Readers Digest Association Limited, 1977

Green, Andrew *Our Haunted Kingdom*, Collins, 1973

Hallam, Jack *The Haunted Inns of England*, Wolfe, 1972

Harper, Charles *Haunted Houses*, Bracken, 1993

Jeffery, P.H. *Ghosts, Legends and Lore of Wales*, Orchard, 1990

Jones, Richard *Walking Haunted London*, New Holland, 1999

Maddox, Brenda *George's Ghosts. A New Life Of W. B. Yeats*, Picador, 1999

Marsden, Simon *The Haunted Realm*, Little, Brown, 1986

Mason, John *Haunted Heritage*, Collins and Brown, 1999

The Parliamentary Gazetteer of Ireland, 1844–45

Playfair, Guy Lion *The Haunted Pub Guide*, Javelin, 1987

Puttick, Betty *Ghosts of Hertfordshire*, Countryside, 1994

Puttick, Betty *Ghosts of Essex*, Countryside, 1997

Seafield, Lily *Scottish Ghosts*, Lomond, 1999

Turner, Mark *Folklore and Mysteries of the Cotswolds*, Hale, 1993

Underwood, Peter *This Haunted Isle*, Javelin, 1986

INDEX

Primary references are in bold.
Page numbers in italics refer to
illustrations.

à Becket, Thomas 23, *23*, 90
Aberglasney House and Gardens
113–114, *113*
Ardvreck Castle **152–3**
Arthur, King 16 *17–18*
Arundel-Radford, Rev. John 23,
23
Ashurst, Sir Trevor 120–21
Avebury 26, *26*, **28–9**

Bagdale Hall **132**, **133**
Ballynacarriga Castle **119**
Barguest (demon dog) 135
Barnes, Mrs. 30–1
Battle Abbey **63–4**, *63*
Bear Inn, The, Stock **72–3**
Belper Arms, The, Newton
Burgoland **88**, *88*
Belvoir Castle 88
Berkeley Castle **40**
Berry Pomeroy Castle **20**, *20*
Birch, Alice 36–7
Bisham Abbey **51–2**
Black Abbot, ghost of Prestbury
41
Black Cat of Killakee, The 125
Black Friar, ghost of Newstead
Abbey 91
Black Horse Inn, The, Pluckley
68
Blackness Castle **148–9**
Blake family 121
Blanchland Abbey 140
Blickling Hall 11
"Blood and the Moon" (W. B.
Yeats) 122
"Bloody Assizes" 19, 32
Boathouse, The, Laugharne
114–115
Bodmin Moor 16, *16*
Boleyn, Anne 10, 37, 49, 59
Borley Rectory **73–6**, *74*, *75*
Bosworth Field 86, *86*
Bosworth Hall Hotel **88**
Bottlebrush Down 26–7, *26*
Bramber Castle **63**
Brown Lady of Raynham Hall
72, 80–1
Brown Man of the Moor 141
Bruce, Robert, King of Scotland
144, 145, 153
Buckland Abbey **20**
Bull, Marianne 74–5
Bull, Rev. Henry 74
Bunyan, John 46
Bury St. Edmunds, Abbey ruins

76–7, *76*
Byron, George Gordon, 6th
Baron (Lord Byron) 90–92, *91*

Cabell, Richard 22
Capesthorne Hall **102–3**
Cappel, the (demon dog) 138
Carlyle, Thomas 146
Castell Coch **112**, *112*
Castle Coombe 31, *31*
Castle Leslie **128–9**, *129*
Castle Rising Castle **78–80**, *78*
Charles I, King 36, 38, 58, 146
Charles Fort **120–21**, *120*
Chattox ("Pendle Witch") 136
Chesterton, G. K. 10
City of Dreadful Night, The (James
Thomson) 45
Clarence, George, Duke of 37
Clay, R. C. 26–7
Claydon House **53**
Clifford, Charles 36–7
Clouds (Rupert Brooke) 70
Clouds Hill **27–8**
Connington **82**
Corfe Castle **28**, *29*
Cromwell, Oliver 58
Crown Inn, The, Bildstone **77**
Culcreuch Castle **149**, *149*
Culpeper, Thomas 60

Dark Angel, The (Lionel Johnson)
85
Darkling Thrush, The (Thomas
Hardy) 56
Darrell, "Wild" Will 31
Dartmoor 16, **20**, **22**, *20*, *22*
Davies, John *110*, 111
Defoe, Daniel 97
Demdike ("Pendle Witch") 136
Dering family 66–7, 68
Device, Alizon 136
Devil's Bridge **109**, **110–111**
Dissolution of the Monasteries
76, 90, 92, 134
"Do Not Go Gentle into that
Good Night" (Dylan Thomas)
115, *115*
Dobbins Inn Hotel **129**
Doncaster, Thomas 92
Douglas, Janet 152
Doyle, Sir Arthur Conan 22
Dozmary Pool **16**, *16*
Dracula, Count 132, *132*
Drake, Sir Francis 20
Dryden, John 107
Dùn an Òir **121**
Dunstanburgh Castle 9, 12,
139–140, *139*
Dunwich **77–8**, *77*

Dysart, Elizabeth Murray,
Countess 58–9
Dysart, William Murray, 1st Earl
of 58

Easter rising (Ireland 1916)
125–6, *126*
Eclipse, The, Winchester **32**
Edgehill **38–9**, *38*, 52, *52*
Edward II, King 40, *40*, 78, 93
Edward III, King 78, 80, 93
Edward IV 40, 50
Edward VI, King 20, 59–60
Edward, Prince 40
Edward the Confessor 63
Eilean Donan Castle **153**
Elizabeth, Queen Mother 150
Elvey Farm Country Hotel 69
Emma, Lady, ghost of Ettington
Park Hotel 39
English Civil War 36, 38, *38*, 41,
42, 53, 67
Ettington Park Hotel **39**, *39*
Eyam **96–7**
"Eye of God" 136

Fairy Steps **137–8**, *137*
Fauld **100**, *100*
Fiends Fell 138
"Five-to-four" Fred, ghost of
Belper Arms 88, *88*
Fleece Inn, The, Bretforton **38**
Flower, Joan, Margaret and
Phillipa 88–9
Forster, Dorothy 141
Forster, E. M. 27, 28
Forster, Tom 141
Fort del Oro **121**
Fosbrooke, Jonas 50, 51
Fotheringay Castle 86, 87
Foyster, Lionel Algernon 74–5

Gates of Remembrance (Frederick
Bligh Bond) 19
George, ghost of Goat Gap Inn
134, *134*
George IV, King 81
George and Pilgrim Hotel, The,
Glastonbury **18–19**, *18*
Gerald the "Wizard Earl" of
Kildare 128
Gibbons, Grinling 104
Glamis Castle *144*, **150–2**, *150*
Glastonbury 16, 18–19
Goat Gap Inn, Settle 134, *134*
Godden, Rumer 65
Goodrich Castle **36–7**, *37*
Goodwin Sands, Deal *58*, **65–6**
Gray Lady of Capesthorne Hall
103

Gray Lady of Crown Inn 77
Gray Lady of Glamis Castle 152
Grey, Lady Jane 49
Grimston, Lady Anne 55
Guildhall, Coventry **93**, *93*
Guy, Sir, the Seeker 139–40

Ham House **58–9**, *59*
Hampton Court Palace 10, 11,
58, **59–60**, *60*
Handel, George Frideric 126
Hand of Glory, The (R. H.
Barham) 130
Hardy, Thomas 27, 56
Harold II (Godwinson), King 58,
63–4, *63*
Hastings, Battle of 58, 63–4
Haunch of Venison, The, Salisbury
29–30
Haunted Houses (Henry
Wadsworth Longfellow) 94
Haunted Palace, The (Edgar Allan
Poe) 35
Haunting of Hill House, The
(Shirley Jackson) 39
"Haunting, The" (Richard Jones) 5
Hell Fire Club 124
Henry II, King 23, 90
Henry VI, King 37, 40, 49
Henry VIII, King 49–50, 58, 59,
60
Hermitage Castle **144–5**
Herstmonceux Castle **64–5**, *64*
Hickling Broad **80**
Highgate Cemetery **46–8**, *48*
Hoby, Dame Elizabeth 51–2
Hoby, William 51–2
Hopkins, Robert Thurston 81
Hound of the Baskervilles, The
(Arthur Conan Doyle) 22
Howard, Catherine 10, 11, 60

Image House **103**, *103*
Isabella, Queen 40, 78, *78*, 80, 93

James I, King of England (James
VI of Scotland) 87, 146
James II, King of England (James
VII of Scotland) 19, 32, *32*, 150
James V, King of Scotland 152
James, Henry *64*, 65
Jarman (landlord of Ostrich Inn)
52–3, *52*
Jay, Kitty, grave of **22–3**
Jeffreys, George (Judge Jeffreys)
19, 32, *32*
John, Augustus 121
John, King 28, 58, 62, *62*

Killakee House **124–5**

Killiecrankie **150**, *150*
Killua Castle *118*, **128**
Kilmainham Jail *124–5*, **125–6**, *126*
Kinder Scout *96*, 99

Lady Lovibond (schooner) *65*, 66
Lairre, Mary, ghost of Borley Rectory 75–6
Lamb, Lady Caroline 91
Lamb House, Rye 65
Lancaster, Thomas, Earl of 139
Lapford Church **23**, *23*
Laud, William 42, *42*
Lauderdale, John Maitland, Duke of 58–9
Lawrence, T. E. ("Lawrence of Arabia") 27–8, *28*, 122
Leap Castle **122–3**, *123*
Leigh, Augusta 91
Leigh, Molly 100–101, *101*
Lilleshall Abbey **104**
Linlithgow Palace **146**
Lisgar, Lady 88
Lisle, Dame Alice 32, *32*
Littlecote House Hotel **30–31**, *30*
Lollards 100
Long Meg and her Daughters **138**, *138*
Longdendale **97–9**, *99*
Lord, Rev. Kenneth 134, *135*
Lord Crewe Arms, The, Blanchland **140–1**
Lovell, Francis, 1st Viscount 41
Luds Church, Gradbach **100**
Lyme Park, Disley **104**, *104*

Macbeth (Shakespeare) 150, *150*
Magna Carta 58, 62, 63
Margaret of Anjou 40, *41*
"Marianne Messages" 75, *75*
Marshall, Charlie 72–3
Martinsdale, Harry 134–5
Mary, Queen of Scots 86, 87, *87*, 104, *104*, 146, *147*
Mary King's Close **147–8**
McAssey, Tom 124, 125
McGill, Dan 125–6
Merlin 17–18
Mermaid's Cove 17
Mermaids Pool **99**
Mill Hotel, The, Sudbury **78**, *78*
Miner's Arms, Eyam 97
Minsden Chapel, Hitchin **54–5**
Minster Lovell Hall **41–2**
Mompesson's Well, Eyam 97
Monmouth, James Scott, Duke of 19
Monmouth uprising 32
Morte d'Arthur, Le (Thomas Malory) 15
Mortimer, Roger, 1st Earl of March 40, 78, 80, 93

Netley Abbey **32**
Newby Church **134**
Newstead Abbey **90**, *91*
Norfolk, Duke of 78

Nottingham Castle 93
Nutter, Alice 136

O'Carroll family 122–3, *123*
Oedipus (John Dryden and Nathaniel Lee) 107
Old Ferry Boat Inn, The, Holywell **82–3**, *82*
Olde Trip to Jerusalem, Ye, Nottingham *91*, **92**
Ostrich Inn, The, Colnbrook **52–3**, *52*
Owlpen Manor 40, *41*
Oxford 36, 38, 42, *42*

Parnell, Charles Stewart 126
Parr, Catherine 41
Parsonage Wood, Castle Coombe **31–2**
Pendle Hill **136**, *136*
Phantom Bomber of Longdendale 97, 99
Phantom Drummer of Herstmonceux Castle 65
Phillips, Thomas 113
Pilgrim's Progress, The (John Bunyan) 46
Plague Cottages, Eyam 96–7, *97*
Plas Mawr **109–110**
Pluckley 58, **66–9**
Pole, Margaret, Countess of Salisbury 49
Polesworth 102
Potsford Gibbet **80**
Powlet, Andrew 86
Prestbury *36*, **41**
Price, Harry and Fanny 112
Price, Harry (founder, National Laboratory of Psychical Research) 74–6, *74*
Princes in the Tower 37, 50, *50*
Priory of the Blessed Virgin Mary, Prittlewell **76**

Ragged Stone Hill **37**
Ramsey, Sir Arthur 144–5
Raynham Hall *72*, **80–81**, *81*
Reculver Towers 68, **69**
Red Lady of St Nicholas's Church, Pluckley 67, *67*
"Remember" (Christina Rossetti) 155
Renwick **138–9**
Richard III, King 37, 49, 50, 86, *86*
Riverside Inn, The, Bovey Tracey **23**
Robber's Grave **111**
Rollright Stones **42**
Rosslyn Chapel, Roslin 146, *147*
Royal Stag, The, Datchet **53**, *52*
Rufford Abbey **92–3**
Rufus Stone **33**, *33*
Rutland, 6th Earl and Countess of 88–9

St. Bartholomew's Church, Warleggan 18
St. Botolph's Church, Bishopsgate

48, *48*
St. Clair, Sheila 124
St. Clair, Sir William, Prince of Orkney 146–7
Saint Editha 102
St. Govan's Chapel, Bosherton **108**
St. John's Church, Burslem **100–1**
St. John's College, Oxford 42, *42*
St. Mary Magdalene's Church, Hucknall Torkard 92
St. Mary the Virgin, Marston Moreteine 54
St. Mary's Church, Reculver *68*, **69**
St. Mary's Church, Woodford 86, *87*
St. Mary's Guildhall, Coventry **93**, *93*
St. Mary-the-Virgin, Bottesford 86, **88–9**
St. Michael's Church, Edmonthorpe **89**, *89*
St. Michan's Church, Dublin **126–8**, *126*
St. Nicholas's Church, Montgomery 111
St. Nicholas's Church, Pluckley 67, *67*
St. Peter's Church, Tewin **55**
St. Ronan's Well (Sir Walter Scott) 39
St. Senara's Church, Zennor 17
Sandwood Bay **153**
Savile family 92
Scholar, The (Robert Southey) 143
Scott, Michael 138
Scott, Sir Walter 39, 146, 152, 153
Sedgemoor Battlefield **19**, *19*
Seymour, Edward 20
Seymour, Jane 59–60, *60*
Shakespeare, William 12, 150, *150*
Shaw, George Bernard 27, 121
Shiel, Isabelle (Tibbie) 146
Shipwrights Arms, The, Faversham 68, **69**
Silent Pool **60**, 62, *62*
Skirrid Mountain Inn, The, Llanfihangel **111–112**, *111*
Smith, Dame Anne 89, *89*
Smith, Rev. G. E. 74
Smith, Sir Roger 89
Smithill's Hall, Bolton **137**
Snell, Johah 80
Snowshill Manor **41**
Spencer, Parson 101
Springhill **129**
Stevenson, Robert Louis 146
Stoker, Bram 132, *132*
Stolen Child, The (W. B. Yeats) 116
Stonehenge (Thomas Stokes Salmon) 25
Strathmore and Kinghorne, "Beardie," Earl of 150
Styles, John 86, *87*
Sunex Amures (spirit) 76

Talbot family 92
Talbot Hotel, The, Oundle **87**, *87*

Tallantire, John 139
Tamworth Castle **102**, *102*
Tanner, Captain Landon P. 98, *98*
Taplin family 38
Tar, Jack, ghost of Shipwrights Arms 69
Tennyson, Alfred, Lord 16
Tewkesbury, Battle of 40
Tewslie, Juliet 82–3, *82*
Thomas, Dylan 114–5, *114*
Thomas, Florence *114*
Thomas of Reading (Thomas Deloney) 52
Thoor Ballyee, Gort **121–2**, *122*
Thornton Abbey, East Halton **90**
Tibbie Shiel's Inn, St. Mary's Loch **146**
Tintagel Castle 16, **17–18**
Tollemache, Lyonel 58–9
Tone, Theobald Wolfe 126
Tower of London *46*, **49–50**, *50*
Townsend, Lord Charles 80–81
Tracey family 23
Treagle, Jan 16
Treasurer's House, York **134–5**, *135*
Trewhella, Matthew 17
Trollers Gill **135**
Tyrrel, Sir Walter 33

Under Milk Wood (Dylan Thomas) 115

Verney, Sir Edmund 38, 53, *53*
Vicars, George 96, *96*

Wade, Charles Paget 41
Waldengrave family 75
Wallace, William 144
Walpole, Dorothy 80–1
Ware, Great Bed of **50–51**, *51*
Warleggan **18**
Warrender, Colonel 120–21
Warrender, Wilful 120–21
Wars of the Roses 40
Wem Town Hall **104**, *104*
Whaley, Richard "Burnchapel" 124–5
Wharton, Lord 81
Whitby Abbey *132*, 133
White Lady of Castell Coch 112, *112*
White Lady of Rufford Abbey 92–3
White Lady of St. Nicholas's Church 67, 68
Wicken Fen **83**, *83*
William I ("the Conqueror"), King 28, 33, 49, 58, 63–4, 102
William II (Rufus), King 33, *33*
Windsor Castle 63
Winter's Gibbet **141**
Wiseman, Dr Richard 10
Wolsey, Cardinal 37, 59
Wood, John 103
Wynne, Robert 109–110

Yeats, W. B. 10, 116, 121, 122

ACKNOWLEDGMENTS

Many people have helped with the research and development of this book. Staff at the numerous local libraries helped me locate ghost stories and haunted sites in their districts. Custodians, guides, and other staff at the historic properties happily updated me on the latest facts concerning their hauntings, or shared with me their own personal experiences. Landlords, bar staff, and customers at old inns and taverns not only gave me the necessary information on their premises but also, on many occasions, pointed me toward other haunted places in their neighborhood and even arranged for me to meet those who had seen the ghosts. People all over Britain and Ireland frequently saved the day by going out of their way to direct me to the places I was seeking when I'd become horribly lost! To all of you I offer my sincere thanks.

At New Holland Publishers I would like to thank Jo Hemmings for her unstinting encouragement and Alan Marshall for his evocative design. Personally I wish to thank Geraldine Hennigan and Mamie Byrne who assisted with research. I wish to pay a warm tribute to the memory of Tom Byrne, whose warm Irish lilt and wonderful tales were always an inspiration. I would like to thank my wife, Joanne, who patiently listened to my stories and supported me throughout the project and my son, Thomas George Jones, who proved as fearless a ghost hunter as any two-year-old can be. I'd also like to thank Dan and Georgia O'Donoghue for their assistance with haunted Ireland. And finally to all those whose stories, be they tragic or otherwise, have made this book possible, long may you wander, but may it always be at peace.

PHOTOGRAPHIC ACKNOWLEDGMENTS

All photographs from The Fortean Picture Library except:
Private Collection/Bridgeman Art Library p38 (bl); Private Collection/Bridgeman Art Library p40 (c); Fitzwilliam Museum, Cambridge/Bridgeman Art Library p42 (c); Royal Holloway and Bedford New College, Surrey/Bridgeman Art Library p50 (t); Victoria & Albert Museum, London/Bridgeman Art Library p51 (tr); Christie's Images/Bridgeman Art Library p56; Kunsthistorisches Museum, Vienna/Bridgeman Art Library p60 (t) Britain on View p31 (tr); p48 (tl); p52 (tl); p87 (tr); p92 (bl); p112 (bl) Castle Leslie p129 Collections/James Bartholomew p44 Collections/Michael Diggin p120; p122 Collections/Robert Hallmann p79; p148 (b) Collections/Image Ireland/Alain Le Garsmeur p124; p126 (c) Collections/Robert Pilgrim p62 (t) Collections/Clive Shenton p102 (tr) Collections/Robin Weaver p94 Culcreuch Castle p149 (tr) Eye Ubiquitous p103 (br) Hulton Getty p121 Richard Jones p17 (tc); p22 (tl); p52 (br); p69 (c); p82 (b); p83 (b); p89 (t); p92 (tr & br); p100; p113 (br); p134 (tl); p137 (br); p141 (br); p150 (bl) Mary Evans Picture Library p28 (c); p65 (tr) Simon Marsden/The Marsden Archive p13; p24; p61; p70; p74 (t); p75 (br); p90; p91 (tr); p116; p123; p127; p133; p145 (t); p151 National Trust/Andreas von Einsiedel p105 National Trust/Nick Meers p59 (t) Pictor International Ltd p49 (tr); p64 (tl) Skibo Castle p152 (bl) William Smuts p160

t = top; b = bottom; c = center; l = left; r = right

While every effort has been taken to ensure that all suppliers of photographs have been credited, New Holland Publishers would like to apologize for any errors or omissions that may have occurred.